Schooling America

Schooling America

America

HOW THE PUBLIC SCHOOLS MEET
THE NATION'S CHANGING NEEDS

Patricia Albjerg Graham

OXFORD
UNIVERSITY PRESS
2005

OXFORD
UNIVERSITY PRESS

Oxford University Press, Inc., publishes works that
further Oxford University's objective of excellence
in research, scholarship, and education.

Oxford   New York
Auckland   Cape Town   Dar es Salaam   Hong Kong   Karachi
Kuala Lumpur   Madrid   Melbourne   Mexico City   Nairobi
New Delhi   Shanghai   Taipei   Toronto

With offices in
Argentina   Austria   Brazil   Chile   Czech Republic   France   Greece
Guatemala   Hungary   Italy   Japan   Poland   Portugal   Singapore
South Korea   Switzerland   Thailand   Turkey   Ukraine   Vietnam

Published by Oxford University Press, Inc.
198 Madison Avenue, New York, NY, 10016
www.oup.com

Oxford is a registered trademark of Oxford University Press

Library of Congress Cataloging-in-Publication Data
Graham, Patricia Albjerg.
   Schooling America / Patricia Albjerg Graham.
      p. cm.
   Includes index.
   ISBN-13: 978-0-19-517222-5
   ISBN-10: 0-19-517222-1
   1. Education—United States—History—20th century.
   I. Title.
   LA209.G65   2005
   370'.973'094—dc22   2005008495

9 8 7 6 5 4 3 2 1
Printed in the United States of America
on acid-free paper

Contents

Illustrations

Acknowledgments

Finding what to include in a book and deciding what it means are the essential steps of historical writing. These are the author's responsibilities, and I accept them, including whatever errors or misinterpretations persist. Elizabeth City, who is completing her doctorate at the Harvard Graduate School of Education, has contributed to this project in countless ways with her sparkling intelligence, remarkable skill at finding obscure items, and seemingly effortless good humor. For nearly fifteen years, Wendy Angus has assisted me (as well as several other faculty members) with grace, accuracy, and reliability for which I am enormously grateful. Research librarians, archivists, and administrators, particularly Katherine Markee, special collections librarian at Purdue University, as well as several staff at Franklin College have also been very helpful. Most of all, thanks to the Harvard Graduate School of Education's superb research librarians, especially the incomparable Patrice Moskow.

Many students, faculty, school practitioners, researchers, parents, and citizens have increased my understanding of various elements of the American educational scene, both past and present. Here I want to give special thanks to Blanche Brick, Anthony Bryk, Michael Caprio, Richard Chait, David K. Cohen, Yves Duhaldeborde, Chester Finn, Howard Gardner, Milton Goldberg, Claudia Goldin, Marguerite Graham, Elisabeth Hansot, Nathan Hardee, James Harvey, Paul Hill, Jennifer Hochschild, Harry Judge, Daniel Koretz, Ellen Condliffe Lagemann, Sara Lawrence-Lightfoot, Marvin Lazerson, Deborah Leff, Richard Light, Bridget Terry Long, Mary Patterson McPherson, Katherine Merseth, Richard Murnane, Jerome T. Murphy, Susan Blankenbaker Noyes, Gary Orfield, Robert Peterkin, Diane Ravitch, Julie Reuben, Robert Schwartz, Marshall Smith, Catherine Snow, Catharine R. Stimpson, David and Edith Tatel, Michael Timpane, David Tyack, Carol Weiss, Patricia White, Keith Whitescarver, John Williams, Ellen Winner, Lillian Wright, and William Wright.

In addition to the assistance of those listed above, I have also revisited some of the material included in my previous books and articles, including *Progressive Education from Arcady to Academe* (New York: Teachers College Press, 1967); *Community and Class in American Education* (New York: John Wiley, 1974); *S.O.S.: Sustain Our Schools* (New York: Hill and Wang, 1992); with Richard Lyman and Martin Trow, *Accountability of Colleges and Universities* (New York: Columbia University Press, 1995); "Women in Academe," *Science* 160 (25 September 1970): 1284–1290; "Carleton Washburne: A Biographical Essay" in Robert Havighurst, ed., *Leaders in Education* NSSE Yearbook (Chicago: University of Chicago Press, 1971); "Schools: Cacophony about Practice, Silence about Purpose," *Daedalus* (1984): 29–57; "Assimilation, Adjustment, and Access: An Antiquarian View of American Education," in Maris Vinovskis and Diane Ravitch, eds., *Learning from the Past: What History Teaches Us about School Reform* (Baltimore: Johns Hopkins University Press, 1995); "Educational Dilemmas for Americans," *Daedalus* (1998): 225–235; "Educational Reform—Why Now?" *Proceedings of the American Philosophical Society,* 146: 3 (September 2002): 256–263; and "The Long Haul," *Education Next* (Spring 2003): 20–23.

While working on this book, I have realized that I would never have written it if Kathleen Hall Jamieson and Jaroslav Pelikan of the Annenberg Institutions of Democracy project had not made an arrangement with Oxford University Press's trade division and its executive editor, Timothy Bartlett, to include public schools as one of the five volumes in their series and then talked me into writing it. I have appreciated their invitation and suggestions. I also thank the staff at Oxford University Press for helpful assistance in the final transition from manuscript to book.

My longest, deepest and most important conversations have been with my husband of more than fifty years, Loren R. Graham, for whom the American public schools provided a path from poverty through a state university to professorships at Columbia University, MIT, and Harvard University. A goal of writing this book has been to help schools and colleges do as well by others as they did by him.

Schooling America

Introduction

SCHOOLS IN AMERICA have danced to different drummers during their long history. Sometimes the drumbeat demanded rigidity in all programs; sometimes it wanted academic learning for only a few. Sometimes it encouraged unleashing children's creativity, not teaching them facts. Sometimes it wanted children to solve the social problems, such as racial segregation, adults could not handle. Sometimes it tacitly supported some schools as warehouses, not instructional facilities. Sometimes it sought schooling to be the equalizer in a society in which the gap between rich and poor was growing. Sometimes the principal purpose of schooling seemed to be teaching citizenship and developing habits of work appropriate for a democratic society, while at other times its purpose seemed to be preparation for employment, which needed the same habits of work but also some academic skills. Now, the drumbeat demands that all children achieve academically at a high level and the measure of that achievement is tests. The rhythm and tempo of the drumbeats have shifted relatively frequently, but the schools have not adjusted to the new musical scores with alacrity. They are typically just beginning to master the previous drummers' music when new drummers appear. Many, though not all, of the new beats have been improvements both for the children and for the nation.

All drummers have sought literacy in English for American children, though very modest literacy levels have been acceptable in the past. Drummers have always sought a few students who attained high levels of academic achievement, including children from disparate social, economic, and racial backgrounds. Beyond that consensus, however, what we have wanted from schooling has changed dramatically over time. These expectations for schools typically have been expressed through criticisms—often virulent—of current school practices, and the responses that followed inevitably were slower and less complete than the most ardent critics demanded. These are the shifting assignments given to schools.

The following chapters of this book describe these shifting assignments given to schools and then to colleges during the last century: "Assimilation: 1900–1920"; "Adjustment: 1920–1954"; "Access: 1954–1983"; and "Achievement: 1983–Present." Each goal has been partially reached, although never as quickly nor as completely as its proponents wished. Certainly this is true of the current one, achievement, for we are reminded daily of the academic inadequacies of our youth. The fifth chapter, "Autonomy to Accountability," inserts into this discussion of schooling the experience of American colleges and universities over the last century. Many Americans believed until the middle of the twentieth century that completing high school sufficed for schooling. During the last half-century, however, we have come to believe that schooling is not complete without college, and a majority of our high school graduates now pursue post-secondary education. College is becoming nearly as universal as high school was in the mid-years of the twentieth century. Colleges have become the schools for adults and now exhibit much the same range of accomplishments and difficulties as do the elementary and secondary schools.

The story begins with the schools' response to the need to assimilate hordes of European immigrants' children at the beginning of the twentieth century and continues to the present demand to assure the academic achievement of all students. American schools and colleges have valiantly, though sometimes reluctantly, adapted their institutions to meet the needs expressed by their critics. In this democratic nation schooling became the core upon which Americans have relied to assure the continuity and evolution of their government, their economy, and their social values. Since authority to maintain the nation resides with the people, not a monarchy, church, or military, then the people must be imbued not only with knowledge but also with virtue in order to assume that profound responsibility. As early as 1816 Thomas Jefferson warned, "If you expect a nation to be ignorant and free and in a state of civilization, you expect what never was and never will be."

In Jefferson's time few supports existed to eliminate ignorance and promote freedom and civilization. Schools seemed the best institutional bet to accomplish this formidable civic task. By the early twentieth century American schools led the world in providing opportunities for instruction in both academic subjects and civic values.

American schools moved gradually and hesitantly in the first half of the twentieth century away from serving the nation's needs toward serving children's needs. Both, of course, are necessary. Early on we sought through schooling to unify the country's population by instilling a primary allegiance to the United States and by teaching skills to enable prosperity. By the 1920s we shifted our emphasis to schools that sought primarily to help children grow up. Increasingly these institutions rejected the excessive rigidity of the formal curriculum and developed teaching methods that emphasized children's interests and social development, sometimes without ensuring the mastery of traditional subject matter. For children in families with rich cultural resources of their own the lack of academic emphasis in school was not harmful, but for children without such traditions, it was devastating, depriving them of access to knowledge.

By the middle years of the twentieth century, critics, including both the literate public and professors, assailed the academic weaknesses of much schooling, designed as it was to foster the "life adjustment" of many American youth. Unlike in Europe, where all but the academically inclined left school by adolescence, in America the majority of students completed secondary school, so a rigorous academic curriculum was seen by some American educators as beyond the reach of most students. Academic critics and hopeful parents demanded access to special programs for "gifted and talented" students. Others demanded access as well, particularly blacks who sought admission to schools from which their children had been lawfully excluded on the basis of their race. Access to enhanced instruction in schools with many low-income students became codified with the first major federal education act in 1965. Additional pressure for access to special arrangements intended to equalize opportunity mounted for bilingual children, for handicapped youth, and, finally, for girls previously excluded from boys-only sports.

Critics reemerged in the early 1980s, now led by businessmen who found themselves confounded in competition with Japanese and European companies and who attributed some of their difficulties to the academic inadequacy of their workforce. Broad coalitions of business leaders, public policy spokespersons, academics, and educators called for strengthened academic instruction for all American youth, particularly for those, often poor and minority, whose test scores trailed affluent Americans and many Europeans and South Asians. How universal academic achievement was to occur immediately without substantial changes in the adolescent youth culture, which no one seriously advocated, or without a fundamental reorientation of school life, which few successfully defined, became the conundrum of the times. It remains so today.

The dilemma for school people, thus, has been how to respond to the public's different and sometimes conflicting demands upon the schools. On the whole, the American people have believed the schools are theirs, and they, not the teachers or administrators, are the ones who should establish priorities for the schools. Public education in America has meant that the public controlled the schools, and the schools should thus serve the public's needs. This conviction that the public should control education stems from Jefferson's observation that a democracy is dependent upon a knowledgeable and virtuous public.

Achieving a knowledgeable and virtuous public has not been easy. Traditionally we have been satisfied with the excellent academic performance of a few, including some rich and a few poor, some white and a few of color. For the remainder we have settled for much more modest academic achievements. Yet for nearly all we have emphasized the "virtue" dimension of the curriculum, stressing fair play, honesty, loyalty to the country, respect for others, teamwork, and, occasionally, ingenuity, creativity, and even kindness. For the first half of the twentieth century this mix served us reasonably well. America became a world power during World War II, after all, when only a tiny fraction of our children had achieved academic eminence and when the United States had few leading research universities of international standing.

But at the beginning of the twenty-first century, Americans are concentrating their educational energies on improving the academic achievement of all our youth. Were that genuinely to happen it would be a wondrous accomplishment both for the youth and for the society. Somehow we hope that greater academic achievement will bring us a more productive society and perhaps even one that is more just. It is hard to imagine, however, how higher test scores alone will do that. Schools that are reorganized to engage and support all children in successful learning as well as schools that themselves exemplify the virtues that we have sought to imbue in the young do have such possibilities. Creating such schools and providing them for all children is our present challenge. Our democracy demands that we meet this challenge.

In America we are deeply indebted to our educational institutions for developing the population that makes our nation work. Yet, we are ambivalent about their contribution, unsure how many of our national successes and failures are attributable to our children's schooling. Certainly schooling can be influential, but even more significant in youths' development is the education they receive in their homes, their communities, and through the media. Those influences, while more important, are much more difficult for a society to regulate, and thus our attention remains upon the educational institutions, whose policies we can regulate but whose practices are vastly more difficult to change.

_____

ONE

Assimilation
1900–1920

A LIVELY, TOWHEADED, EIGHT-YEAR-OLD BOY shivered with dread and excitement on a cool morning in September 1900 in Ottertail County, Minnesota, as he headed for his first day of school. His older brother, Mads, and his older sister, Esther, had already attempted this venture, and neither had liked it at all. For many, not only the first day of school but latter days as well were a harrowing experience. Subsequently his six younger brothers and sisters would make the same journey, and most of them would not like it either. His father offered one piece of advice in Danish, the only language spoken in the family, "When the teacher looks at you, stand up and say, 'My name is Victor Lincoln Albjerg.'" That was his preparation for schooling in America. His parents' concession to his need for Americanization was his middle name; they offered few others. Victor Lincoln Albjerg was my father.

Little Victor followed his father's advice precisely, and when the teacher turned to him, he rose and replied as his father had instructed. Derisive laughter

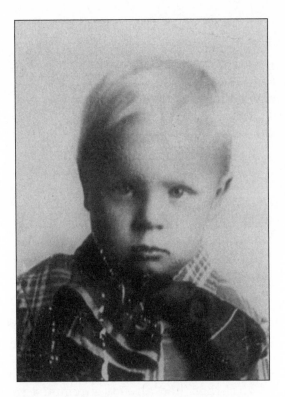

My father, Victor Lincoln Albjerg, 1900.
Courtesy of Patricia Albjerg Graham

from his fellow students and a frown from the teacher greeted him. Confused and embarrassed, he sat immediately, and understood why Mads and Esther had sought to avoid school. Obviously the teacher had asked him something other than his name, but, since she spoke English and he spoke only Danish, he had no idea what she had said. The teacher, on the other hand, recognized that her preeminent task was to teach her pupils English, and to do so she forbade them from speaking their family language to each other in the school or schoolyard. The sharp rap of the birch rod met such infractions.

Despite his inauspicious beginning, Victor prospered in the school, more than his father wished. Victor's father believed in schooling only within "thrifty limits," by which he meant a modicum of English and arithmetic and perhaps a bit else but not enough to give students an appetite for further book learning that might take them away from their local environment. As his father feared, Victor, unlike his brothers, did not want to return to the family farm. As he expressed it, "I wanted to be somebody—a rural schoolteacher." In 1909 at the age of seventeen he became one, earning forty dollars per month for the three-month term at a nearby one-room school.

The nine Albjerg children exemplified what most Americans then wanted the schools to do: assimilate youngsters into American life. Fundamentally the curriculum was the same for native-born and immigrant children, though the latter had the additional obstacle of learning English as a foreign language rather than as their native tongue. And there were lots of immigrant children eligible for schooling as between 1890 and 1920 more than 18 million people came to the United States, largely from eastern and southern Europe, where few had experienced significant schooling. Many, though not all, saw their children's schooling as the primary means of success in their new land.

The immigrant youngsters presented an immediate concern because their families could not be counted upon to instill either the English language fluency or the values associated with American patriotism that native-born, white families were assumed to provide. Thus, many Americans considered schooling for immigrants even more important than for others, an expectation seen most vividly in the South, where schooling for white, native-born youth was substantially less than that provided in other parts of the country where immigrants settled in much larger numbers. Blacks in the South, of course, had even fewer educational opportunities.

Most Americans, both native born and newly arrived, thought that only a few children needed extended education, and only one Albjerg, Victor, received it. But all needed familiarity or, at least, acquaintance with the English language, with American customs and "patriotic lore," some arithmetic, as well as with traditions of honesty, hard work, and fair play. This was the curriculum of assimilation, promising all children both virtue and knowledge with greater emphasis on the former than the latter.

Such schooling then sufficed to provide students with the skills to participate as citizens and to support themselves. Seven of the nine Albjerg children remained in Ottertail County for most of their lives, a common pattern. Yet despite their lack of extended schooling, all were self-sufficient, even frugal Esther, who never married and spent her entire life speaking Danish, caring first for her parents and then for other elderly neighbors.

On the whole the system worked well. The schools' role was to meet the needs of the society by preparing children for participation in it. The needs of children were subordinated to the needs of the society. Generally schools did not consider seriously children's social, psychological, or even academic development, and expected them to adapt to the routines established by the school. That would all change by the 1920s when the reaction against school rigidity prompted a profound shift of school focus from the needs of the society to the needs of children.

The mix of virtue and knowledge seemed about right for the early twentieth century. To help students attain these goals the schools increasingly engaged in hidebound instructional practices that many children found unappealing, as Victor's brothers and sisters did.

Most left these unappealing institutions after only a few years of attendance. That was what both Americanization and assimilation meant, a little schooling for a lot of children.

AMERICANIZATION AS ASSIMILATION

William Torrey Harris, U.S. commissioner of education, forcefully alerted his fellow citizens to the challenges that mass immigration brought in 1877: "If we do not 'Americanize' our immigrants by luring them to participate in our best civilization . . . they will contribute to the degeneration of our political body and thus de-Americanize and destroy our national life." "Americanization" was a process, much as vulcanization of rubber was: conversion of a raw product into a tough, durable, usable, valuable good that benefited the whole society.

Harris's views dominated American expectations for education well into the twentieth century as a 1912 article in the *Wall Street Journal* explained:

> Our public schools are filled with a conglomerate mass of foreigners and children of foreigners sprung from generations of ignorance and untrained intelligence. To make good citizens of these through a few years of schooling is a stupendous task. Anything that can be devised to enhance mental and physical condition, which as a rule carries with it moral tone, should be considered worth trying. What this country needs at this time more than all else is the elevation of its citizenship.

Elevating the mental and physical condition of the young with some additional moral tone became the curriculum of assimilation.

On the assumption, and it was a big one, that the immigrants and their children wanted to become "Americanized," then this curriculum benefited them as well.

The individuals who made the arduous emigration to the United States, however, came for a variety of reasons, particularly poverty or political or religious discrimination in their homelands. America for them offered the opportunity to build a better life, certainly for their children and possibly for themselves. Such entirely legitimate reasons for emigrating did not mean, however, that they wished to give up their native language, cuisine, customs, and religion, what we would call today their culture. That was the tension Victor Albjerg's father, Niels, expressed when he spoke of schooling within "thrifty limits." The old Dane wanted his children to get enough book learning at school in order to get by in America but not so much that they would exchange the primacy of their family identity for a more cosmopolitan American identity. Some other immigrants sought more educational opportunities for their children, but Niels was not alone in favoring limited learning.

Native-born white Americans generally agreed that assimilating other white immigrants was an urgent national priority. Distant memories of the difficulty of melding the thirteen original colonies into one nation persisted. More recent memories of the fratricidal Civil War reminded Americans of the importance of gaining the loyalty of residents and potential citizens to the United States.

As early as the 1840s, the Massachusetts commissioner of education Horace Mann had argued vigorously and persuasively that public education in the common school was desirable both for America and for Americans. Many people north of the Mason-Dixon line agreed with Mann. What Mann and his supporters meant by "common" was that the schools be universal, enrolling all children, both those of the "common people" (the poor) as well as those of the leaders of the community, and providing a similar curriculum for all. Until Mann's time, children of affluent families typically attended schools that charged tuition while children of the poor enrolled in "charity schools." Mann wanted the support of all families for their children to study in "common schools," subsidized by taxes.

The "common" school being considered at the time was almost exclusively what we would today call an elementary school, so the issue of a universal curriculum was not as controversial as it would become when later educators considered what to teach in high schools. The thrust of Mann's argument, which he began articulating before the massive immigration of the late nineteenth century, was that publicly supported schools needed to be improved and needed the support of the affluent in the community, not just the poor. Mann invoked competition with the Prussians, considered the best-educated people in Europe, to stimulate American interest and compliance. Public education needed to become the standard for the nation, Mann argued, not various private schools driven by assorted ideologies and economic interests. This argument echoed that of the Founding Fathers, namely that a democracy relying on the will of the people needed to be sure that the people were both informed and loyal or the nation itself would suffer.

When massive numbers of Europeans immigrated from various countries beginning in the 1890s, common schools, as public schools were often called, were well established in cities, towns, and in most northern rural areas. Typically they concentrated on the first eight grades with most students dropping out before completion. They did, however, provide the basics of English literacy for those students who spent some time in them.

Americans at this time were moving in increasing numbers from rural areas to towns, where more schools were available and where many jobs required higher levels of literacy and numeracy and the habits of punctuality, teamwork, and accommodation to institutional structures, each of which was considered a "virtue." From the nineteenth to the twentieth century, a nation that had been made predominantly of small business people, farmers, and people who worked the natural resources of the land and sea (loggers, fishermen, miners) became an urban, industrial society, which required substantially more skills and attitudes taught in schools. By 1920 half of the U.S. population lived in communities of 2,500 or more, and three-quarters of the immigrant population resided in cities. Administrators of large cities, such as New York, Chicago, Boston, or Detroit, estimated that two-thirds to three-quarters of their populations were either foreign born or children of foreign born.

Many immigrants remained in rural areas, particularly the Scandinavians and Germans who settled in the Midwest. These groups were less in the public eye and, therefore, triggered less nativist concern about assimilation than did their immigrant brethren from southern and eastern Europe. The latter were likely to be Roman Catholic or Jewish and to have come with limited educational attainments and even less money. As they were the most numerous, the most different, the most needy, and, especially, the most visible to journalists at major newspapers in cities, they were the focus of the assimilationists' attention. Some programs existed to help adults adjust to their new home, but the focus and the hope was for the children.

Political leaders, clergy, journalists, and the public generally agreed on which institutions of the society should lead in the effort to assimilate the immigrant population and which should not. Schools were to accomplish this effort while other entities remained bastions of immigrant homogeneity. Neighborhoods remained constellations of ethnic compatriots. Ethnic, non-English-language newspapers grew in number and variety as different national groups arrived, thus validating the family language as a means of communication even in America. Religious institutions remained significantly ethnically homogeneous with Irish Catholics worshiping at St. Patrick, Germans at St. Boniface, Italians at St. Anthony, and Poles at St. Casimir. German and Scandinavian Lutherans divided their devotion among different churches, many of which used the language of the old country for their liturgy, thus reinforcing the division not only between Germans and their northern neighbors but also among Norwegians, Danes, and Swedes. Eastern European Jews established their own congregations and did not find themselves welcome at the services of their more prosperous and better established German co-religionists. These various religious institutions served not only as places of worship but also in many cases as community centers where persons of similar ethnicity, speaking the language of their childhood, could gather in this new, strange American setting to enjoy the familiar cuisine of sauerkraut or kielbasa or aebleskivers. By the beginning of the twentieth century many of these churches had established their own parochial schools, and in large cities, such as New York, a few distinctive Jewish schools had been organized.

If local communities, newspapers, churches, and synagogues perpetuated the language and religious and cultural traditions of immigrants, what institutions were left to engage in the Americanization process? Clearly the emerging and rapidly growing public school system and later (during World War I) the military filled this need. The schools, first, taught English and attempted with partial success to make students of all ethnicities literate in it; second, acquainted them with emerging American patriotic lore; and, third, provided some initial preparation for work. The heroic tales of historic American figures collected in the popular McGuffey Readers were the source of the "patriotic lore." Acquainting students with American culture was at least as important as teaching English, and was vital to instilling citizenship. While the patriotic program served both native-born and immigrant children, the emphasis upon mastering English and prohibiting use of the family language was arduous for the immigrants. But the assimilation agenda for immigrants also fit Americans' expectations for native-born whites. In fact, the convergence of what was needed for Americans and what was needed for immigrants made the assimilationists' task easier than it would have been if separate curricula had been deemed necessary.

As had been the case in discussions of education in the eighteenth and nineteenth centuries, the implicit goal of publicly funded schooling, which was often supplemented by private tuition, was to strengthen the state by creating a citizenry that could participate effectively in the democratic process. This need was as acute for native-born whites as for immigrants. By the mid-nineteenth century, under Horace Mann's leadership, effective participation in the democratic process implied acceptance of certain moral standards, ones that schools were expected to inculcate.

The Founding Fathers' Enlightenment goals for education in the new democracy had been knowledge and virtue, building as they did on Puritan values in which both were valued equally. But as the new government

---

Facing page Released by the board of education in Cleveland, Ohio, and available in six languages, including English, Italian, Polish, and Yiddish, this 1917 poster encouraged immigrant parents and children to learn English in America's public schools. *Smithsonian Institution Collections, National Museum of American History, Behring Center, Division of Home and Community Life*

CLEVELAND
MANY PEOPLES, ONE LANGUAGE

Come to the Public Schools
Learn the Language of America.
Prepare for American Citizenship.
Free Classes for both Men and Women.
Classes in the Evening and Afternoon.
Apply to nearest Public School or
  Library for further information.

Venite alle Scuole Pubbliche
Imparate la linqua di America. Preparate
  di diventare un cittadino Americano.
Ve ne sono classe per nomini e donne.
Le classe· sono serali ed anche dopo
  mezzogiorno.
Andate alla scuola pubblica pui vicina o alla
Biblioteca pubblica per altra informazione.

Jöjjenek a Public Schoolokba
Tanulják meg Amerika nyelvét.
Készüljön amerikai polgárnak.
Osztályok ugy férfiak mint nök számára.
Elöadások délután es este.
Jelentkezzék a legközelebbi iskolában
vagy könyvtárban bövebb felvilágositásert.

Pridite v ljudske Šole!
Učite se ameriškega· jezika!
Pripravljajte se za državljanstvo!
Razredi za moške in ženske!
Poduk zvečer in popoldne!
Vprašajte v bliznji publik šoli ali v
  čitalnici za nadeljna pójasnila.

Zapisz się do Szkoly Publicznej
Ucz się języka angielskiego.
Przygotuj się do Obywatelstwa
  tego kraju.
Otwieramy klasy dla mężczyzn i kobiet
  wieczorami i po poludniu.
Zgloś się do najbliższej Publicznej Szkoly
  lub Biblioteki po dalsze informacye.

קומט אין פאבליק סקוהל.
לערנען די אמעריקאאנער שפּראך.
זיך פֿארבערייטען צו אמעריקאן סיטיזענשיפ
פֿרייט קלאסען פֿאר מענער און פֿרויען.
קלאסען אין אבענד אויך נאכמיטאג.
ווענדעט זיך צום נאהנטסטען סקוהל אדער
לייבררארי פיר ווייטערע אויסקינפטען.

BOARD OF EDUCATION
EAST SIXTH AND ROCKWELL
IN CO-OPERATION WITH THE
CLEVELAND AMERICANIZATION COMMITTEE
(Mayor's Advisory War Committee)

was put into action new needs became evident. The nation had to govern itself through citizen participation, which required informed and honorable men. The new nation was also far more heterogeneous than Puritan New England had been, and thus a new, inclusive national identity must be forged. The Philadelphia physician Benjamin Rush published his "Thoughts upon the Mode of Education Proper in a Republic" in 1786, arguing "We have changed our forms of government, but it remains yet to effect a revolution in our principles, opinions, and manner so as to accommodate them to the form of government we have adopted." Rush saw schooling principally as a means of assuring competent citizens, startling today's readers with such sentiments as "Let our pupil be taught that he does not belong to himself, but that he is public property" or "I consider it possible to convert men into republican machines."

By the end of the eighteenth century the universal emphasis on knowledge had declined while the emphasis on virtue had increased with particular attention to standards familiar to Protestants, though not exclusive to them. Many Americans expressed alarm about the habits, customs, and values that the immigrants, most of whom were not Protestant, were bringing with them to the United States. Thus, the emphasis on virtue, which adopted the essence of Protestant rhetoric, stressing honesty, hard work, and fair play, seemed particularly appropriate. Further, the limitations of American democracy in the late nineteenth and twentieth centuries, including but not limited to racial segregation and machine politics, led people to seek virtue in the young because it was so lacking in their parents. Give the problem to the schools, many argued, rather than try and change the habits, behaviors, and views of the grown-ups.

In 1900, Americans understood that theirs was a nation that characterized itself as a democracy, though its unity had recently been challenged by the Civil War, by Reconstruction, and now by large numbers of foreigners who sought to live here. The nature of democracy meant that the populace, both citizens and citizens-to-be, had a voice in its destiny. Schoolteachers and administrators understood that their job was to assure that the predominant voice was virtuous; a little but not much knowledge would suffice for most.

THE SEPARATE SOUTH

One region, the South, did not undergo urbanization and immigration, and blacks, a high fraction of its residents, were denied fundamental rights of citizenship. Therefore, the southern story of schooling differed significantly from that of the rest of the country. Put simply, there was much less of it for whites and even less for blacks.

The South remained predominantly poor and rural in the first two decades of the twentieth century while the rest of the country embarked on major growth of towns and cities. Public funds were scarce, and needs were great, thus reducing the amount available for public education. Schools floundered in rural areas where the population concentrations were small, where publicly subsidized transportation was not available, and where the jobs were predominantly agricultural and did not seem to require much formal study. Furthermore, white immigration to the South was very low, thereby eliminating one stimulus to schooling, preparing non-English speakers for citizenship. Finally, and most important, when schooling was seen as primarily serving the needs of the society to prepare citizens, few whites wished to spend much of their limited funds on schooling for their black neighbors, who, despite the post–Civil War amendments to the U.S. Constitution, still did not enjoy full rights as citizens.

The consequences of diminished educational opportunities became evident in literacy rates in the South, where the highest fraction of white native-born illiterates in America lived in 1910. In general, the illiteracy rate for blacks was much higher than for whites, and the majority of blacks lived in the South. School enrollment in the northeast quadrant of the nation in 1910 hovered around 90 percent of the six to fourteen year olds while in the South it was about 70 percent and significantly lower (56 percent) for southern blacks. The consequence of the lack of support for publicly funded schooling in the South became evident during World War I, when 17 percent of Alabama draftees were classified as illiterate in English (despite their nearly all being native born) compared with a national figure of 7 percent. Black draftees from the North scored higher than white draftees from Alabama.

Except for a few northern white philanthropists, whites generally did not argue forcefully to educate blacks. Both Booker T. Washington and W. E. B. DuBois, as well as blacks in their local communities, spoke eloquently about the educational needs of their people. Washington sought schooling that would prepare blacks for the kinds of employment they were likely to find while DuBois argued for a classical education that would make them academically competitive with the best-educated whites. In a predominantly rural society where the skill requirements for employment were minimal and where citizenship rights were not available to blacks, the white community did not choose to invest significantly in their education.

Alabama, for example, typically ranked near the bottom in most educational measures. Neither black nor white Alabamians were served well by their separate school systems. Alabama did not have many immigrants in need of Americanization to stimulate educational efforts as they had in the North. Alabama had less than 1 percent foreign-born residents in 1910, compared to nearly 15 percent nationally. Nonetheless, in Alabama this small group of foreign born led the state in 1910 in sending its children to school (78 percent versus 70 percent of children aged six to fourteen of native-born whites and 50 percent of blacks). The rest of the country was expanding its school year and increasing students' attendance, while Alabama and other southern states followed suit but at a much slower pace. In 1919 Alabama had a 132-day school year for whites (black students' school year was only 102 days) with an average of 46 days attended. In contrast, the New York State school year at the time was 190 days with an average of 154 days attended. In Michigan, another heavily immigrant state, students had a 172-day school year with 140 days attended. Indiana, more southern in outlook and less heavily immigrant, had a 155-day school year with 127 days attended. Today the typical school year is 180 days.

The most egregious disparity in educational opportunities in the South in the twentieth century was the gap between what was offered to whites and what was offered to blacks. Again, Alabama is illustrative. During the Reconstruction Era through 1890, white and black teachers' salaries were very low but roughly equitable (twenty-three dollars a month for white teachers and twenty-two dollars a month for black teachers). Beginning in the early 1890s the Alabama legislature passed new laws declaring that state funds for education no longer needed to be distributed proportionately to the races. The state superintendent of public instruction explained that "colored" children "in general [are] only capable of receiving and profiting by an elementary education which costs comparatively much less than that suitable for the white race in its more advanced stages of civilization." By 1910 white teachers were earning an average of fifty-four dollars a month and black teachers twenty-four dollars. Per pupil expenditure for whites and blacks followed the same pattern; Lowndes County (a rich agricultural county in central Alabama with relatively few white children and many blacks) spent $33.40 per white child and $1.00 per black child in 1912.

In nearby Butler County, with the change in the funding formula, competing Baptist and Methodist high schools for whites closed and sold their furniture to the new public one being built for them. Meanwhile, blacks in the county struggled to create tiny Baptist and Methodist high schools for their children since no public funding was available for them. In 1916 only two public high schools for blacks existed in Alabama, and they enrolled a total of 224 students. The remaining 1,220 black secondary students attended private high schools, mostly run by Methodists and Baptists. By this time each county in Alabama had at least one public high school for whites, and many had several.

The 1800s began with uncertainty about the ability of the colonies to become a nation, and the Civil War and Reconstruction divided the unity of the county at the end of the century. But by 1900 white southerners had regained control in their states, and legal segregation was becoming deeply entrenched with the passage of Jim Crow laws and Supreme Court decisions, such as *Plessy* v. *Ferguson* in 1896, which mandated separate railroad cars for blacks and whites. In the South, as in the rest of the country, the emphasis in schooling was more on "virtue" than upon "knowledge" except for the very small fraction of students, mostly of whites, who anticipated a college education. Thus was nationhood maintained, though questions could be raised about democracy.

TEACHING PATRIOTISM

The extraordinary growth of school enrollment in the United States outside of the South, from 17 million students in 1900 to more than 23 million in 1920, mirrored the pattern of immigration. Immigration did not cause this growth alone, however. Many immigrants came to towns and cities, where the concentration of people made it easier to establish schools than in scattered rural areas lacking good transportation. Further, journalistic accounts, such as those of Jacob Riis in New York City, and social settlement reports, such as those of Jane Addams in Chicago, brought to public attention the large numbers of immigrants whose children were perceived to "need" Americanization in the schools. This need somehow seemed less pressing in rural Alger County with its many immigrant families along the southern shore of Lake Superior where journalists and social workers seldom ventured.

With the dramatic increase in immigration from 1890 to 1910 concentrated in urban neighborhoods and made visible by newspapers and social reform groups, school men in American cities felt the pressure to respond. While some thought may have been given to the interests and welfare of the schoolchildren themselves, the force behind their effort was the national perception that these youngsters must grow up as patriotic Americans. While widespread agreement existed on the role of the schools in assimilating the youth, both immigrant and white native born, no comparable agreement existed on the means by which this should occur. Nor was there agreement about the kind of patriotism that was desirable.

Today, scholars describe the competing views with greater complexity and nuance than was articulated at the time. "Cosmopolitan patriotism" is the term of art favored by contemporary historian Jonathan Hansen to describe the views of philosopher John Dewey, social settlement leader Jane Addams, and philosopher W. E. B. DuBois, among others. Hansen cogently argues that they believed "the proper object of patriotic loyalty was not the American nation-state, but the ideal of democratic social reciprocity for which the nation-state was a vehicle." Hansen's distinction eluded the early-twentieth-century school men who believed that saluting the Stars and Stripes and understanding that America was the greatest nation in the world was what the children needed.

As Hansen suggests, John Dewey and his high-toned colleagues had much more subtle notions of patriotism in mind, ones that recognized the obligations of both the citizen to the state and of the state to the citizen, including the citizens' responsibility to serve the state through their enlightened criticism of it. For the beleaguered school administrator, however, a more simplistic goal seemed appropriate.

While all three of these powerful figures influenced what Americans thought their schools should do, few ordinary Americans could or would have articulated patriotism as they did. Many undoubtedly would have agreed that the democratic values America embraced rhetorically, if not always in practice, and the opportunities such democratic values provided were the nation's most valuable assets. Many immigrants came to America particularly, rather than some other place, because of those very values. The ability to dissent from the government without retribution, to criticize authority without penalty, lies at the core of American social thought.

Education through its manifestation in early-twentieth-century schooling, however, found these democratic ideals very difficult to uphold in practice. Most schoolteachers and administrators did not welcome either dissent or criticism of their authority. Early-twentieth-century American schooling put a premium on obedience and on following the rules. This emphasis was thought to be necessary for and beneficial to children (though it certainly made a teacher's life easier as well) as they prepared for adulthood, when they would be expected to function according to society's norms. Children everywhere have been punished for infractions of school rules regardless of whether the rules were just or not. Typically they have not been encouraged to question the rules.

Despite the high-minded discussions of reformers such as Dewey, Addams, and DuBois, schooling is not about talk. Rather, it is about practice, about what children experience in school, and it is in the world of practice that the democratic values have been most at risk. Practice often requires simplification of complex ideas. The "cosmopolitan patriotism" of Dewey, Addams, and DuBois identified by Hansen is one such complex idea. Thus, it was not surprising that many educators approached the need for creating patriots as well as the role of the school in assimilation through more comprehensible tasks than instilling the "ideal of social reciprocity." Who knew what that might mean or how one should do that?

The school superintendent, overburdened with too many students, too few competent teachers, too little money, and too few grown-ups who could understand the languages the children spoke, laid down the rules and expected the teachers to make the children follow them. Such actions fit well with the emerging "scientific management" movement, the proponents of which sought to systematize operations and make them efficient. School administrators strove to make their schools work, not to encourage insightful advances in either virtue or knowledge on the part of students.

To accommodate these realities teachers became absolute authorities; English was the only school language; only unconditional expressions of loyalty to the

United States were permitted; and students remained in a grade (often for several years) until they mastered the curriculum. Eventually a differentiated high school curriculum emerged for those considered unable to master the traditional college preparatory one. Above all, schools sought punctuality, perseverance, hard work, and honesty, not traits universally displayed by the young. Children learned poems (Henry Wadsworth Longfellow's "Paul Revere's Ride") and songs ("My Country 'Tis of Thee") that honored America, and when school lunches became available, the cuisine was, like the language, Anglo-American. Milk, baked fish, and canned pears replaced the pasta, pickles, or borscht of students' homes. Patriotism in many schools was reduced to a bland commitment to the symbols of Anglo-America.

The patriotic curriculum reinforced the values the native-born white children received through their homes or neighborhood institutions and was an obligatory introduction for the immigrants. The child who was fluent in English and who came from a family that either had experienced formal education or who valued learning might be expected to progress more smoothly through the public school system than an immigrant child whose parents' literacy was limited in any language and who knew no English.

Differences in accomplishment resulting from family background seemed natural, though clearly there were many exceptions to it, including native-born children who did not progress and immigrants who did. New York City revealed such a disparity in its high school enrollments in 1908, when 32 percent of children of native-born whites enrolled in school while 13 percent of children of immigrants from non-English speaking countries did. Other cities revealed similar patterns: Chicago with 42 percent and 18 percent, Philadelphia with 27 percent and 13 percent, and St. Louis with 27 percent and 10 percent. Boston, often an outlier in educational matters, followed the same pattern but with higher participation rates: 70 percent and 38 percent.

American school men widely agreed with the sentiment of the New York City school superintendent who defined the goal of school "to teach an appreciation of the institutions of this country and an absolute forgetfulness of all obligations or connections with other countries because of descent or birth." Educators had accepted the challenge to assimilate the immigrant children in their schools. When World War II began a generation later, the descendents of European immigrants were regarded as fully Americanized. However, the children of Japanese immigrants, a different racial group from the dominant Caucasians who had been the focus of assimilationist efforts, were not, and second generation families were placed in internment camps. The government questioned their loyalty to the United States. Apparently, Americanization was for whites only.

Assimilation did not come easily. Three issues dominated attempts to realize it. First, there was a dramatic growth in population and hence in enrollments, making it necessary to accommodate many more children in schools. Second, the high school evolved from serving the few to the many with consequent changes for curriculum, and, third, testing technology was invented to legitimize decisions sorting students into particular educational programs.

EXPANSION AND ITS CONSEQUENCES

Expansion nearly overwhelmed schooling in the first two decades of the twentieth century. The growth came in several ways. There was an increase in the number of children enrolled, an increase in the number attending school regularly, and an increase in the number of grades completed. This was coupled with a broadening of the school program to include many nonacademic activities, such as school lunches, supervised after-school play, or medical services, as well as the evolution of what came to be known as "extracurricular" activities, such as sports, music, yearbook, and theater programs.

While most schools experienced these changes, they were most prevalent in the northern urban schools, which enrolled concentrations of immigrant youth. These schools and their students remained in the public eye in large part because of the proximity of articulate reformers with access to the media of the day: newspapers, pulpits, and community centers. These reformers effectively pushed the schools to change. These schools also benefited from better trained teachers and administrators than those in rural areas and often from students whose immigrant parents strongly motivated them "to make something of themselves" through education as that was their principal resource. Most remarkably by 1920 city schools were frequently considered the best in America, though typically not those serving entirely immigrant constituencies. The best were often ones with a predominantly Protestant clientele with some bright and highly motivated immigrant students. Furthermore, in the big cities, such as New York and Chicago, social settlements, libraries available to the public, and other—often religious—institutions augmented the educational mission of the schools, particularly for the immigrant community.

The best schools were blessed with good teachers, many of them women whose gender precluded them from most professions and often impecunious men who spent some years teaching before completing their own education. Teaching was often a first step on the professional ladder for recent immigrants, both male and female, who had mastered English. For women it was generally the only step, but for many white men it was the first in a sequence.

As the numbers of children attending school increased, the most immediate response by bewildered school men was to reorganize the school, which had generally not divided pupils by age, into grades. In rural schools, such as Victor's in Ottertail County, Minnesota, all youngsters sat together in the same room, taught by a single teacher, who managed to make some of them literate in English, and who gave them some fundamental introduction to reading, arithmetic, patriotic stories, and little else. When Victor became a teacher in 1909, his preparation for teaching mostly consisted of making a favorable impression on the local township trustee who hired him. Eventually he would have to pass an exam. Thus his career in education continued, teaching rural schools in Minnesota with one year of high school work at the closest normal school (institutions to prepare teachers that generally became state teachers colleges), in Moorhead. In 1912, the year he attended, the bulletin of the school described its mission, "The great majority of the youth in our state do not advance beyond the elementary schools, and it is this great population which the normal school, through its product, is called upon to prepare for citizenship."

Such career trajectories understandably worried adults who were concerned about the quality and what came to be known as the "professional qualifications" of teachers. Clearly Victor had few of the latter when he began teaching, and his background was typical of many beginning teachers in rural and many town schools.

By the early years of the twentieth century even relatively small towns were likely to have high schools, normal schools, or small colleges in which individuals could

Victor Lincoln Albjerg (middle row, center) with his eighth-grade graduating class in rural Ottertail County, Minnesota, 1908. For most of his classmates, graduation marked the completion of schooling. *Courtesy of Patricia Albjerg Graham*

receive more extensive education before presenting themselves as teachers. My mother, Marguerite Hall, graduated from Franklin High School in the county seat of Johnson County, Indiana, in 1913 and from the local college, Franklin College, four years later, unburdened by any courses in pedagogy. She began her teaching career in tiny Woodburn, Indiana, followed by jobs teaching high school in Lawrence, Kansas, and Lebanon, Indiana. Her pupils were nearly all native-born whites while Victor's were primarily white, recent immigrants. This was common both then and now: the more extensively prepared teachers taught the children who had the greatest educational resources in their homes and communities and the least prepared teachers taught the children with the fewest resources.

In the cities, however, programs to prepare teachers flourished because the need was so clear. Established on the inauspicious site of the Morningside Heights insane asylum in New York City, Teachers College, located next to and in affiliation with Columbia University, quickly became the national leader of such institutions. Organized in 1887 and initially led by Nicholas Murray Butler, Teachers College dominated the study of education and its practice for the first half of the twentieth century, providing much of the faculty for newly founded departments of education at other major universities. Furthermore, for the first half of the century it was the undisputed leader in the nation—and perhaps the world—in defining the profession of education and preparing its practitioners.

Teachers in cities, particularly New York, faced an intense growth in numbers of children to be served. From a population of 1.5 million in 1890, New York City had exploded to a population of 5 million in 1915. The school year frequently opened with as many as thirty thousand more students than desks in the schools. By 1910 more than twice as many residents were foreign-born as were native-born of native parents. There were nearly twice again as many who had either one or both parents born abroad. In short, it was an immigrant city, predominantly white with 2 percent nonwhite. In 1920 approximately 35 percent of the population was Roman Catholic, another 35 percent Protestant, and 29 percent Jewish. Observing her community, Lillian Wald, a leader of social settlements in New York at the time, commented, "The stronghold of our democracy is the public school. This conviction lies deep in the hearts of the social enthusiasts who would keep the school free from the demoralization of cant and impure politics and restore it to the people, a shrine for education, a center for public uses."

Whether the new breed of professional educators could accomplish such an ambitious task remained to be seen. These professionals counseled the burgeoning schools to become systems, and they readily offered advice on how to organize their often-chaotic operations. They adapted the new ideas of emerging management specialists Frederick Winslow Taylor and Frank Gilbreth, whose studies of time and motion among industrial workers taught the nation that profound efficiencies could occur with systematization. Henry Ford understood that he could produce his uniformly black cars more efficiently by using an assembly line and making each car identical. Most of the populace did not take in the concurrent finding that as efficiency increased so did workers' stress. The managerial differences between assembly line production and the education of children did not surface immediately among the enthusiasts of administrative efficiency. The new professional educators adopted the findings of Taylor and Gilbreth for the schools and their systems, hoping to gain "efficiencies" through social engineering.

Many on the Teachers College faculty embraced what they termed "the cult of efficiency." David Snedden, for example, envisioned the "social engineering" that large schools could promote. His colleague Edward L. Thorndike developed tests, heralding them as advances in the "scientific measurement of learning." Education professionals focused upon organizational strategies for managing schools consistent with public goals for them, particularly assimilation. Meanwhile, across 120th Street from Teachers College, John Dewey had joined the Columbia University faculty in philosophy and had begun work on his 1916 magnum opus, *Democracy and Education*, which explained education not in terms of efficiency but rather in terms of "growth." The two concepts did not blend smoothly, an indication of difficulties to come.

Historians David Tyack and Elisabeth Hansot have described how the public expected professional educators to become "managers of virtue." Subsequently many Americans have criticized, sometimes severely, the efforts of professionalization that created impenetrable bureaucracies that often seemed to benefit the adults, not the children, and to separate the schools from the communities they served. But faced with the numbers and with the needs of schoolchildren, particularly in predominantly urban and immigrant America, the effort to impose a system on chaos was irresistible for a nation that was searching for order, historian Robert Wiebe observed.

The first "efficiency" was the graded school, which permitted educators to indulge their fantasy that if you grouped thirty to sixty children of the same age in one room they could all be taught and learn the material at the same rate. Soon that notion was dispelled, and instead the graded classes began with children the same age and, as the grades advanced, many children who had failed to learn the material of the grade during the year were held back, often for another unsuccessful year. Sometimes the children failed because they did not show up regularly in school; sometimes they failed because they were neither in the mood to learn nor equipped linguistically to master the material; sometimes they were simply "slow." In New York City the percentages of "over-age" children rose with each grade. For example, in 1904, with the new administrative capacity that permitted school-wide accounting, New York reported the following percentages of "over-age students": 23 percent in first grade, 38 percent in second grade, 45 percent in third grade, and 49 percent in fourth and fifth grades. Later grades had lower rates as the children simply quit enrolling in school. Whatever the reason, there were lots of such children nationally, the majority in fact, as Leonard Ayres documented in his 1908 classic, *Laggards in our Schools*. Ayres observed that of 1,000 children entering city schools, many of which were the best in the country, only 263 would reach eighth grade and a mere 56 the fourth year of high school. His figures for rural schools, particularly in the South, were much lower.

Graded schools did permit, however, the new breed of administrators to get an organizational handle on the hordes of ill-prepared children they were supposed to educate. While the problem was acute for immigrants in the cities, the county seats with native-born populations were not immune from it, either, as Marguerite Hall's school in Franklin, Indiana, reveals. When her older siblings entered the school, which served whites only, in the 1890s the school had so many first grade students (undoubtedly many repeaters) that it conducted classes in two sessions. Sixty-six students came in the morning to study with a single teacher and another sixty-nine came to her in the afternoon. Such numbers precluded much individual attention and necessitated considerable regimentation. By grade two the enrollment had shrunk to fifty-seven. About 11 percent of the students who began graduated from high school, which had been established in the 1870s in this educationally advanced community. The local school serving blacks also experienced deep losses between grade one (twenty students) and grade two (eight). By grade eight only four students remained. From 1898 to 1918 two black teachers taught all the grades; one of them (the man) also served as principal. Yet amazingly Indiana's public schools produced some of the nation's leading white education scholars in the early and mid-twentieth century, including the first dean of Stanford's School of Education, several leading faculty members at Teachers College, and the leading proponent of "life adjustment education" of the 1940s.

Expansion, then, in numbers enrolled and attending and in grades completed, brought monumental challenges to the educators assigned responsibility for these children's schooling. On the whole, they met expansion by enlarging their schools, eliminating the one-teacher schools (which decreased from 200 per 1,000 in 1916 to 149 per 1,000 in 1930), and by consolidating schools. All these changes were touted as improvements, and some undoubtedly were beneficial for the children's education. Some, however, were not. Ultimately the preferred solution was sorting, placing students in classes with others of similar achievement, a technique that helped beleaguered educators deal with their excessive numbers of pupils and inadequate resources but failed to provide for many children the lively and intellectually expansive education they deserved.

EVOLUTION OF THE HIGH SCHOOL

High schools have a mixed history. Until the beginning of the twentieth century they were seen primarily in relationship to colleges, often as "prep schools." In the South and parts of the North they were often termed "academies" and those that served girls from affluent families were called "finishing schools." In all cases they bore closer kinship to higher education than to elementary schools.

Luther Short, the editor of the Johnson County, Indiana, *Democrat,* had in fact argued in 1884 that the few local students requiring post-elementary education be sent to the preparatory department of the local college, Franklin, rather than attend the public high school, which Short found wanting academically and unnecessarily burdensome to the taxpayers. (He did not add that this infusion of students would also help the struggling college, where one of his favorite relatives was professor and vice president.) His view did not prevail, largely because of the dramatic increase in post-elementary enrollments beginning at the turn of the century. By no means all of these students intended to go to college, but Short's proposal does exemplify the limited commitment to public high schools even in the American heartland at the end of the nineteenth century.

Presidents of leading colleges, concerned about declining enrollments in the late nineteenth century, recognized that strengthening the high schools in their states would benefit their institutions. Some, such as the new state universities in Michigan and Wisconsin, favored the development of local public high schools, whose certified graduates were then assured admission. Princeton, however, eschewed the New Jersey public high schools and concentrated upon aiding Lawrence-ville and other local private prep schools.

Charles William Eliot, president of Harvard from 1869 to 1909, led the higher education community's efforts to work with the schools. Eliot, originally a chemist, chaired the National Education Association's Committee of Ten on Secondary School Studies. The committee's 1893 report argued, to the consternation of the classicists, for a common curriculum, including modern foreign languages and scientific studies, as opposed to one dominated by Latin, Greek, and other classic subjects. At the time of the report less than 5 percent of seventeen-year-olds completed high school, so the institutions remained focused on the few. Under such circumstances, when there were only slightly more than 250,000 high school students, a common curriculum for all seemed plausible.

In 1876 a court decision based on a Kalamazoo, Michigan, case had permitted expenditure of public funds for high schools, not just "common schools." These new institutions, which grew slowly and were concentrated particularly in northern cities and county seats, attracted a broader set of students than the "prep" schools. The percentage of students graduating from high school would nearly triple from just 6 percent of seventeen-year-olds in 1900 to 17 percent in 1920, almost 2.5 million students. Clearly a policy intended for 250,000 students might not be appropriate for a student body nearly ten times that size and growing rapidly. What to do?

"The institutions of . . . education in any nation are always a faithful mirror in which are sharply reflected the national history and character," Charles William Eliot had said in his inaugural address as president of Harvard in 1869. However, by 1908, Eliot recognized that the secondary schools were serving a very different clientele than had been the case when his Committee of Ten began its deliberations in the early 1890s. Thus, Eliot developed advice both for Harvard's benefit and also for what he considered sound national policy. In 1908 he urged a policy quite different from the common curriculum for all high school students advocated by the Committee of Ten. Speaking to an emerging professional group—the National Society for the Promotion of Industrial Education—Eliot argued, "The teachers of the elementary school ought to sort the pupils and sort them by their evident or probable destinies."

Both teachers and administrators found solace and legitimacy in this recommendation. Sorting students gave teachers a new authority and administrators a means by which to deal with the phenomenon of their burgeoning numbers of pupils, who clearly were not homogeneous in their rates or styles of learning. The solution of the graded school clearly would not work at the high school level, just as it was not functioning smoothly at the elementary level as the high drop-out rates and massive retention in grades revealed. The older the children became the more they differed in their academic accomplishments. Few fourth graders were four years behind in their school work, though many eighth graders were four, five, or six years behind while some of their classmates were two, three, or four years ahead. Thus, the range of academic proficiency and interest for high school age students, roughly twelve to eighteen, was vast indeed.

But, as this administrative efficiency of "sorting" became routine, what were the fundamental criteria by which teachers could sort? Existing academic achievement was clearly one criterion, but the most obvious sorting mechanisms were gender, race, ethnicity, and, to the extent to which it could be inferred (and it was relatively easy to do so in many cases), wealth. Academic achievement as measured by mastery of the nineteenth-century curriculum was a most unreliable estimate of academic potential for immigrant youth for whom school progress was obviously hampered by their lack of English facility or sometimes by familial obligations. For a society committed to the principles of democracy and opportunity, such sorting could be problematic, particularly if the criteria were not perceived as fair. Thus, the need accelerated to create programs within the schools that were thought to be both beneficial and fair. From these forces came vocational education.

What came to be known as vocational education had many origins. Throughout the nineteenth century the work of various European educators, particularly the Swiss Johann Pestalozzi and later the Italian Maria Montessori, had emphasized that children's learning was enhanced by touching and actively engaging in the subject to be studied. The German-American Felix Adler introduced the Swedish method of *sloyd,* or handwork, in the late nineteenth century in America, where it soon evolved into a tradition known as manual training. Literally, of course, this meant teaching the hand to be productive. In the late nineteenth and early twentieth centuries, John Dewey, Scott Nearing, Francis Parker, and others who advocated such active learning, as manual training came to be known, believed it was beneficial for all children—an additional sensory experience that would facilitate learning beyond the traditional language-based curriculum. Clearly for immigrants it was advantageous to have a way to learn and to display one's accomplishments that was not based in a language with which one was unfamiliar.

Such active learning, however, required very different teaching styles and school arrangements than the increasingly regimented programs that the administrative efficiency experts who dominated public schooling in the assimilation era advocated. The early advocates of manual training thought they were simply expanding the repertoire of pedagogical strategies and learning tools for all children, rich and poor, native and immigrant. By the 1920s, 1930s, and 1940s, their ideas were widely implemented first in private schools serving the moderately affluent, such as the Ethical Culture Schools that Felix Adler founded in New York City, or in the various "progressive" schools that looked to John Dewey for their inspiration.

In the early twentieth century, however, "manual training" changed its meaning and also became identified with the vocational education movement, which focused on non-college-bound students, a very different constituency than the Adler/Dewey progressive schools. Teachers engaged in rigorous sorting of their students, abetted by administrators who sought to devise programs that would keep students enrolled, and hence increase their enterprise. Both soon realized that instruction in "shop" for city boys could lead to courses in carpentry, thus creating an expanded vocational curriculum. Such courses might be useful for students seeking jobs, and would also preclude the need for the English teacher to instruct these reluctant scholars in *Macbeth*. Many teachers and students found this arrangement mutually advantageous.

Similarly, given the few opportunities for women's employment, courses for girls emerged chiefly in domestic science or home economics, fancy names for cooking, sewing, and cleaning. By the second decade of the twentieth century, instruction in the new secretarial technology, typing, was offered largely to urban girls in what came to be known as commercial courses.

In rural areas the vocational courses for girls were similar as the anticipated destiny for most females was housekeeping, but for the boys, of course, Eliot's "evident or probable destiny" rule dictated instruction in agriculture whether the boy had any proclivity for it or not. Parents such as Victor's father who were eager for their sons to stay on the farm largely supported such programs as most recognized, even in the early years of the twentieth century, that the intellectually expansive experience of further education for a gifted son— even high school but particularly college—would increase the chances that he would not return to the farm. Let him learn about crop rotation, not the rotation of the earth in astronomy.

The high schools that were initially created in cities to offer vocational courses to non-college-bound students became known as manual training high schools. This term persisted well into the twentieth century, particularly in the South, where much of the high school work offered to blacks was through such institutions. As noted above, although the manual training curriculum was intended originally as a means of infusing instruction with greater sensory experience in order to make learning both more interesting and more meaningful, in too many instances it became a euphemism for work experience with minimal instruction either in a farm or shop setting. Most such work was narrowly focused on a specific skill, such as wood working or crop cultivation. This was a cheap way to convey skills to young workers who were consequently deprived of a rich curriculum that would allow them to develop their varied interests. Rather, they spent their time hoeing a cotton patch or building a birdhouse. These activities did not increase literacy or numeracy, but presumably they did exemplify hard work, fair play, and honesty, qualities the adults considered desirable in the young.

Many early-twentieth-century efforts to diversify the high school curriculum to include industrial or agricultural subjects took place locally in an attempt to accommodate the twin problems of the need for a trained work force and the growing and changing school enrollments. City schools led the charge because urbanization and industrialization required skilled labor, which was in short supply. Further, cities had the most immigrants, whose difficulties with the traditional college preparatory curriculum were believed to be most acute. Rural areas outside the South also moved to find ways to make their school programs more attuned to the perceived interests of their constituents. There were numerous examples of local and regional educators acquiescing to the priorities put forth by community leaders. Democracy in education was supposed to work this way: at public expense, educators were to provide programs that representative leadership believed was appropriate for youth.

Enthusiasm for vocational education was widespread. John Gray, head of the economics department at the University of Minnesota, expressed his comprehensive vision in 1914,

So long as the world must work to live, so long must men be trained for their work. That training cannot be obtained outside of the schools. The mass of the people cannot be held in the schools to get any kind of an education unless the public schools are vocationalized. The American public high school must give this vocational training. . . . The next step will be to vocationalize the lower schools in the same way. . . . Have no fear that such a scheme will destroy culture or cause learning, literature, or art to dwindle. . . . It is the only way in which the mass of mankind can be relieved from monotonous and unending drudgery and raised to the rank of citizens.

In short, the only way to keep the hordes in schools was to change the curriculum in ways that would make

Students at the North Bennett Street Industrial School are packed into a classroom in Boston, Massachusetts, which boasted one of the nation's leading school systems, 1917.
The Schlesinger Library, Radcliffe Institute, Harvard University

it more easily understood and more immediately useful, allowing them better jobs, jobs that would make them more productive citizens. Some might question how academic culture would be continued, but once vocationalism took hold it—not literature, mathematics, history, or science—drove school priorities. Preparation for work, not preparation for citizenship, emerged as a principal goal of schooling. Early on, one crucial symbol of this was the salaries of vocational education teachers, which typically were significantly higher than those of regular teachers.

John Dewey, in a 1915 article in the *New Republic*, recognized the dangerous narrowness of business-led legislation that permitted business, not educators, to control vocational education. Dewey criticized state-supported vocational education in Indiana that "deals with the subject matter of the day employment," thus minimizing students' opportunities for job mobility through additional instruction. This article in the *New Republic* triggered an exchange with the advocate of school efficiency and social engineering David Snedden, who vigorously defended vocational education and the role of the business leadership in controlling it. Snedden observed that

> Business men generally are suspicious of the so-called academic mind in connection with vocational education. They feel assured neither of the friendliness nor the competency of our schoolmasters in developing sound industrial education. For that reason they often favor some form of partially separate control, at least at the outset of any new experiment. . . . School men, however well-intentioned, are apt to be impractical and to fail to appreciate actual conditions.

Isaac Kandel, a Romanian immigrant who had become a professor of comparative education at Teachers College, summarized America's torturous efforts to establish federal aid for vocational education in a landmark report in 1917. He observed, "What the country needs at the present moment in education is the guidance of the expert." This sentiment reinforced Snedden's argument about expertise without attending to Dewey's concern for the larger social vision implicit in the advice of such experts. Snedden's and Kandel's views also added to the emerging critique of "school men" as being less competent than businessmen even about educational matters. That critique and conviction about the inadequacy of the adults who taught and administered schools would grow throughout the century, culminating in calls from business to reform the schools at the end of the century.

Eventually, after considerable lobbying, the federal government agreed to pay for teachers who could instruct students in workplace skills. The Smith-Hughes Act, the first major legislation providing federal funds for public elementary or secondary schooling, passed in 1917 with the support of both labor and management. But at least as important as the funding precedent it established was the rejection of a "common curriculum" for all American youth through high school. Segmentation of the high school curriculum, led by vocational education, has plagued instruction ever since. Typically low-income students have found themselves in weak academic environments composed of "general" or vocational courses while other students have flourished or floundered in stronger academic or college preparatory courses.

By 1920 the conviction that all children must learn the same things now ended somewhere around the primary grades, and the notion of equivalence of various school curricula—that one subject was as good as another in providing an education—became legitimate. Students could now get a high school diploma either by studying algebra, geometry, biology, English, history, and a foreign language for four years or by enrolling for four years of shop, vocational agriculture, or home economics, all with a little basic English and general math included. "Knowledge," meaning the mastery of academic subjects, reached only the few while everybody encountered the "virtue" curriculum with its expectations of regular attendance, teamwork, honesty, and hard work.

These changes brought the dissolution of the academic curriculum as it had been known and the evolution of a system in which certain children were "tracked" into academic courses and others into nonacademic or vocational ones. The "sorting" that Eliot had recommended to the elementary teachers in 1908 became the "tracking" of the twentieth century, a fundamental mode of school organization in any school with a large enough enrollment to undertake it.

Perhaps if mass immigration had continued into the 1920s and 1930s, Americans would have been more concerned about making sure that all youth in America were learning a common cultural heritage through the school curriculum. After World War I, immigration nearly ground to a halt in the United States, and concern about "Americanizing" the immigrant abated. When schools were perceived as principally serving the needs of the nation, as assimilation proclaimed, then the state placed a significant priority upon their activities, but when the focus was upon the development of the children themselves, as in subsequent decades, the public voice was quieter.

SORTING THROUGH TESTING: THE MODERN METHOD

For primary grade students (six- to ten-year-olds) considerable consensus about what should be learned existed. In the early years of the twentieth century only in the United States did many students continue beyond those grades. England's notorious "eleven plus" examinations continued until well after World War II, designating which children would conclude their formal education at that age and which might continue on to additional formal study. Because the United States led the world for most of the twentieth century in the percentage of its youth who completed the most years of schooling, it faced early on the need for some legitimate means to determine which courses of study were most appropriate for which students. Other nations would come later to this problem and could benefit from both the successes and failures of the U.S. experience.

The United States did not have national examinations that precluded low scorers from continuing in school, and public opinion increasingly saw value both for the society and for the students in graduating from high school. Therefore, some means was necessary to arrange courses of study that children of different abilities and motivations could complete. The sorting that Eliot had advocated in 1908 must be done in a manner that could pass for fair. The most obvious means of selection by race, ethnicity, gender, or family income needed a supplemental method that met the fairness criterion a little more persuasively.

At the same time that the schools recognized the need for a relatively fair method of sorting, the U.S. military found itself desperately in need of one when mobilization for World War I began. Suddenly large numbers of youthful recruits appeared and required immediate sorting to determine which small fraction might usefully be trained as officers or, more likely, pressed into action as "doughboys" or be declared "unfit to serve" on the basis of low performance.

This dilemma gripped the federal government. How to find a solution quickly? Improbably, the government turned to a group of professors to solve this national problem. Professors providing solutions to national problems seemed highly unusual in 1917. They were professors of psychology, a new specialty in the universities, and the solution they delivered on time for use by the military was the Army Alpha, the first standardized test that allegedly measured innate intelligence. A recruit's "mental age" was determined based on the score achieved. Additional calculations with the "mental age" and actual age led to an "IQ," an abbreviation for Intelligence Quotient. A score of 100 slotted one as normal while 140 indicated a genius. Developed by Robert Yerkes of Harvard, Lewis Terman of Stanford, and H. H. Goddard of the Vineland Institute, the test would determine accurately—they said—the native intelligence of young adults.

What the professors developed was the first paper and pencil test that could be administered to large groups, easily scored, and presumed to measure inherent intelligence accurately. The Army Alpha laid the basis for the "objective" group tests given to schoolchildren broadly after 1920. Such tests were presumed to measure either native intelligence or academic achievement. In the public's mind the distinction between the two was not always clear.

Yerkes, born in 1876, was in midlife at the beginning of World War I, unhappy at Harvard and too old to serve in the military. Eager to do his patriotic duty, he threw himself into the collaborative work of developing the test and promoted it vigorously. After the war, possibly because of his extravagant promises for the Army Alpha, which were later shown to be inflated, Yerkes left Harvard for Yale and returned to studying primates where presumably the measurement of intelligence was a little less complex. Terman, a year younger than Yerkes, was happier at Stanford and after the war he remained committed to the testing of human intelligence. As a professor of education and psychology at

Stanford, he prepared a generation of leading test specialists in America, including Arthur Otis, who developed one of the first and most widely used group intelligence tests for schoolchildren.

H. H. Goddard, who preceded Terman as a doctoral student at Clark University, had joined the staff at an institution for the "feebleminded" in Vineland, New Jersey, in 1906. Two years later he went to Europe, where he encountered the work of two leading researchers, Alfred Binet and Theodore Simon, and their 1905 article, "Upon the Necessity of Establishing a Scientific Diagnosis of Inferior States of Intelligence." His translation of the article became the basis of his work at the Vineland Institute, correlating observational estimates of the residents' abilities with their scores on the Binet/Simon scale. By 1910, Goddard posited that a mental age (MA, as it became known) of 0-2 ranked one as an idiot; 3-7, an imbecile; and 8-12, a moron. These mental ages became crucial to the testing debate.

Goddard and his colleagues labored valiantly and produced the Army Alpha (and a version for those illiterate in English, the Army Beta) in time for its use at the end of World War I. As Yerkes explained,

> Examinations Alpha and Beta are so constructed and administered as to minimize the handicap of men who because of foreign birth or lack of education are little skilled in the use of English. These group examinations were originally intended, and are now definitely known, to measure native intellectual ability. They are to some extent influenced by educational acquirement, but in the main the soldier's inborn intelligence and not the accidents of environment determines his mental rating or grade in the army.

Having thus assured Americans of the legitimate scientific truth of these tests of intellectual ability, Yerkes's and his colleagues' next revelation sobered the public: the average mental age of American soldiers was thirteen. Could a democracy survive with citizens of such limited cognitive development?

Although the research basis for these tests was developed with individuals identified as "feebleminded," Yerkes and Terman, according to the historian James Reed, "regarded their tests as means of liberating gifted individuals from the tyrannies of ascribed status based on class or race or ethnicity. They did not expect . . . to find much gold among the masses." That the tests favored those familiar with American middle-class culture (and hence discriminated against the many who were not familiar with such mores) was most evident in the final section of the eight-part test. Unlike the previous sections, which emphasized vocabulary, numeracy, symbols, and "common sense," Test 8 required knowledge of early-twentieth-century American life. The August 16, 1918, edition inquired whether Yale was in New Haven, Annapolis, Ithaca, or Cambridge; whether Corona was a kind of phonograph, multigraph, adding machine, or typewriter; whether John Wesley was most famous in literature, science, war, or religion; and thirty-seven other questions similarly rooted in American culture. Scores on all eight sections of the test were totaled, and a mental age and IQ were computed. Thus, a person might do quite well on the symbolic, mathematical, and even vocabulary sections of the test and not at all well on Test 8 and, therefore, do poorly overall. Similarly, a student who had picked up the fact that Milwaukee was known for beer and other such cultural tidbits found in Test 8 had a considerable advantage in the final scoring. These kinds of tests rapidly made their way into the schools in the 1920s and 1930s as a means of understanding children's abilities and hence their appropriate curricular placement, with an IQ number assigned to each child's permanent record.

Terman defended his tests for use in schools, invoking their contribution to democracy though a different definition of democracy than cited by earlier commentators: "There is nothing about an individual as important as his IQ, except possibly his morals . . . the great test of democracy is how to adjust itself to the large IQ differences which can be demonstrated to exist among the members of any race or nationality group." Here was a restatement of the tension between virtue and knowledge as goals of schooling.

Many agreed, particularly those who sought "gifted" or "advanced" courses for high-scoring children. Testing increased the pressure to break the academic lockstep that had characterized the efforts of early-twentieth-century school administrators committed to assimilation. They had organized and systematized their schools to accommodate their dramatically increasing enrollments, many of them immigrants. In doing so, they laid the foundation for criticism of their excessive rigidity and disdain for individual differences among their pupils. The critique took form as a new emphasis in schooling: adjustment.

TWO

Adjustment
1920–1954

WORLD WAR I, according to President Woodrow Wilson
and other sloganeers, made "the world safe for democracy." Americans were largely spared the cataclysmic
effects of the Great War endured by Europeans. Nonetheless, the national mood in the United States changed
dramatically, and, as is so often the case, this shift in
sentiments could be clearly discerned in new priorities
for the school system, initially for children of well-
educated and wealthy parents. Pundits proclaimed that
assimilation had been achieved, although the practices
associated with it faded only gradually over the next
two decades and particularly persisted in schools serving immigrant and other low-income children.

America in the 1920s experienced a period of growing wealth, considerable corporate and governmentally
ignored greed, widespread racial and religious bigotry,
and rapidly changing social mores, particularly for ur-
banites. In such a period, discussions about the national
need for assimilation as a means of preserving the democracy seemed out of place. With so much change in

the air, "adjustment" to the new times emerged as the new catchword.

Many of the most salient events and practices of the post–World War I period (the Teapot Dome financial scandal, the rise of the Ku Klux Klan, lynchings of blacks in the South, and the economic depression following the stock market crash of 1929) did not reflect well on the democracy Americans aspired to have. President Wilson might claim that the world was "safe for democracy," but his piece of the world, the United States, did not admirably demonstrate it at the time. Nor, of course, did the new Soviet Russia, recently emerged both from incredible losses in World War I and from the yoke of the czars and now engaging in a different form of authoritarian rule. Germany, principal adversary of the Allies in World War I, entered the 1920s badly broken. The Germans attempted a new and ultimately unstable form of government before acquiescing to Hitler's takeover in 1933, resulting in a devastating defeat of democracy.

As the Roaring Twenties took off, American educators, always anxious to be au courant with what was expected of them, found their old priorities obsolete. Prescient school men recognized that the focus was shifting from schools serving a need defined by the nation (assimilation) to one defined by informed, ambitious, and often affluent parents seeking a more supportive school environment for their children and by newly articulate professors of education. Modern educators in the 1920s turned their attention starkly from schools that would principally serve the needs of the American democracy through the education of the young and instead focused upon the other half of the equation—the children themselves. Hence, the educators made a transition from assimilation, something the nation needed, to adjustment, something the children needed.

The change in emphasis was dramatic: from the poor to the rich; from the immigrant to the native born; from rigid schooling to a flexible curriculum; from the disciplinary subjects of English, mathematics, and science to the arts of music, painting, and dance. As Teachers College professor Harold Rugg and his co-author, Ann Shumaker, later editor of *Progressive Education*, proclaimed in their popular 1928 volume, *The Child-Centered School*, "For education in the Century of the Child aims at nothing less than the production of individuality through the integration of experience. . . . Thus, the vocabulary of the new schools has coursing though it a unitary integrating theme: individuality, personality, experience."

The Progressive Education Association, which had been founded in 1919 and articulated as its aim "the freest and fullest development of the individual, based upon the scientific study of his physical, mental, spiritual, and social characteristics and needs," caught this new wave of enthusiasm. Early leaders of the association, particularly Eugene Randolph Smith and Marietta Johnson, formulated the seven tenets on which school programs loosely organized themselves: "Freedom to Develop Naturally; Interest the Motive of All Work; The Teacher a Guide, Not a Task-Master; Scientific Study of Pupil Development; Greater Attention to All that Affects the Child's Physical Development; Co-operation Between School and Home to Meet the Needs of Child-Life; and The Progressive School a Leader in Educational Movements." Together they encompassed the credo of adjustment.

The children whose needs emerged as paramount were those who came from middle- and upper-class families who believed the schools were too rigid in their curriculum, pedagogy, and administration and who took action to assure that their children would have a superior education. Thomas S. Kuhn was such a child. He

Students construct maps to learn the geography of South America—presumably a more appealing task than reading about the region—at the Lincoln School in New York City, 1942. *Library of Congress, Prints & Photographs Division, FSA-OWI Collection, [LC-USW3-009899-E]*

began his schooling in New York City at the Rockefeller-endowed Lincoln School of Teachers College. When his family moved to the suburb of Croton-on-Hudson, he continued at Hessian Hill School. Both schools were exemplars of institutions that followed the seven tenets of progressivism. Years later Kuhn reminisced about how he had loved school and the freedom and support he had encountered there. School served him well; he graduated summa cum laude in physics from Harvard in 1943 and became one of the leading American academics of the second half of the twentieth century, best known for his book *The Structure of Scientific Revolutions*. For children from families with strong academic and cultural resources and with gifted and imaginative teachers these schools were marvelous; for others without such family supplements and with ordinary teachers, they degenerated into holding pens.

Sensible families have always wanted their children to be happy. Traditional schools of the assimilationist era left many, perhaps most, young people alienated from schools that expected docile behavior and dreary memorization of facts. As children continued in these deadening settings for longer and longer periods of time, now often ten or twelve years instead of only three or four, the challenge to make the experience pleasant, lively, as well as instructive grew. Thus, a key goal of the adjustment era was to provide a school experience that would enhance the youngster's development: psychological, social, physical, moral, civic, aesthetic, and even intellectual. Shaping these sentiments were the new educational elite: professors of education, particularly at Teachers College, Columbia University, who urged emerging school leaders to accept their views.

ENTHUSIAST OF ADJUSTMENT: LUCY SPRAGUE MITCHELL

Leading the effort to devise schools that children would love and that would supplement their rich cultural resources at home was Lucy Sprague Mitchell. Born in 1878 to a wealthy but unhappy Chicago family, Lucy grew up unhappy as well. Her childhood malaise, her family's affluence and cultural sophistication, and her close connections with some of the leading educators of the day would dramatically shape her adult outlook. Because she believed herself to have satisfactorily mastered the academic demands made of her but not the intra and interpersonal ones that troubled her and her family so greatly, she spent more of her time on the latter in developing her educational programs. She assumed that if children's psychological and social development prospered, then inevitably their intellectual development would as well. Better schooling could accomplish both, she believed, and that conviction inspired the "adjustment" curriculum of the next generation. Hers was a grand aspiration, marvelous when fully realized but catastrophic when only partially achieved, as was typically the case.

After graduating from Radcliffe College in 1900, Lucy, like many of her contemporaries, floundered as she pondered marriage or a career, initially believing she must choose between the two. Coming from a well-connected family, she developed many influential friends, particularly in higher education. The new president of the University of California, Benjamin Ide Wheeler, a friend of her brother-in-law, appointed her Berkeley's first dean of women and assistant professor of English, the latter a tribute to her longstanding interest in writing. In the Berkeley community she made many friends, including Agnes Hocking, whose husband, Ernest, was a professor of philosophy who would later help her develop her educational vision. She also re-met an economist, Wesley Claire Mitchell, whom after much angst and indecision she married in 1912. He went on to a very distinguished career as a professor at Columbia University and the National Bureau of Economic Research as a specialist on business cycles and quantification of economic data.

After a seven-month honeymoon in Europe, largely financed by Lucy's inheritance, the Mitchells settled in New York City's Greenwich Village, where they found the intense mix of art, philosophy, psychology, literature, politics, and social reform much to their tastes. When Lucy had initially come to New York in 1911, she had worked with several women leaders in social reform (Lillian Wald, Florence Kelley, Mary Simkhovitch) and in public education (Julia Richman). In addition, she had sought the advice of John Dewey, her family's friend from Chicago, now professor of philosophy at Columbia, and cemented a close, long-lasting friendship with him.

Much in keeping with the assimilationist times of the early twentieth century, she wrote about efficiencies the schools might achieve and the value of testing programs. In addition, she argued for the importance of sex education in the schools. Working with New York City's Public Education Association, she volunteered as a visiting teacher and at their request visited the Gary, Indiana, "platoon schools," which ran with split sessions combining academic study, vocational activities, and home visits by teachers. The Gary schools won plaudits from leading journalist Randolph Bourne and achieved much favorable attention, characteristic as they were of programs for mostly low-income and often immigrant children learning to be Americans in efficiently organized schools.

When Lucy returned to New York City as a wife, she again sought out women leaders attempting to reform the public schools, particularly Harriet Johnson, Caroline Pratt, and Elisabeth Irwin. All would soon give up on the public schools as venues for their educational reforms, finding the bureaucracy—even then—too stifling for their dispositions. Change is always difficult, and efforts to adopt the "Gary Plan" for New York City failed politically in 1917 despite the efforts of Superintendent William Maxwell. Partly as a consequence of that political fight and partly because of its own bureaucratic intransigence, the New York City public school system did not welcome the educational innovations the women attempted. As a consequence, all four turned their energies to establishing private schools that would attract children of well-educated, often affluent families like Mitchell's and embody their educational vision, which encompassed the sentiments of the Progressive Education Association but left teachers considerable leeway to design their own classroom activities.

Having been rebuffed by the public schools, now having children of her own who required good schooling, and having come into another source of family money (from a cousin whose parents had died), Lucy Sprague Mitchell created the Bureau of Educational Experiments in 1916. Like her vision, its mission was vague, but the basic idea was to coordinate and publicize new experiments in education, presumably those that fit her amorphous ideals. The most immediate such project that she supported was her friend Caroline Pratt's City and Country School, which adjoined the Mitchell home. This also became the first school that her four children attended and the place where she taught. Its program for seven-year-olds included play experiences, practical experiences, special training (the only academic activity that included reading, spelling, writing, and numbers), and organization of information. Special training constituted no more than one hour per day, during which shop was also available.

City and Country School, originally called the Play School, was the antithesis of the nearby New York City public elementary schools with their regimented organization and formal curricula. Rather, at the Play

Time	Monday	Tuesday	Wednesday	Thursday	Friday
9.00	Discussion	Discussion	Discussion	Discussion	Discussion
9.20	Rhythms	9.30 Writing	Music	Rhythms	9.30 Number
10.00	{ Shop or Free Period	{ Shop or Science Laboratory	{ Shop or Free Period	Reading	{ Shop or Free Period
11.00	Reading { Shop open	Reading { Shop open	Reading { Shop open	Free Period	Reading { Shop open
11.30	Number { also	Number { also	Writing { also	11.45 { Play in Yard	Writing { also
12.00	{ Play in Yard	{ Play in Yard	{ Play in Yard	12.15 Stories	12.00 { Play in Yard
12.35	{ Lunch and Rest Period	{ Lunch and Rest Period	{ Lunch and Rest Period	{ Lunch and Rest Period	{ Lunch and Rest Period
2.00	Drawing	Stories 2.15 Cooking	Stories 2.20 { Free Period	Drawing or Clay	{ Play in Yard 2.30 Science
2.40	Stories				Music
3.00	{ Play in Yard			{ Play in Yard	
3.30	Home	Home	Home	Home	Home

School founders Lucy Sprague Mitchell and Caroline Pratt
devised the weekly program for privileged seven-year-old
students at the City and Country School in New York City,
1922–1923. The schedule placed more emphasis on creative
activities, such as art and music, than on academic studies,
including reading and math. *Published in Caroline Pratt, ed.,*
Experimental Practice in the City and Country School *(New
York: E. P. Dutton & Company, 1924)*

School children of various ages were expected to "play"
together with various materials (paints, blocks, and
occasionally books) and from this activity derive plea-
sure and perhaps construct meaning. When they were
ready and in the mood, books were available for them
to read, as was some instruction in how to read, if it
was necessary. For the youngsters this unstructured
time in the company of thoughtful and insightful teachers and, generally, in the company of other children
from homes of highly educated and sophisticated parents could be delightful. A New York City classroom of
forty children, with a single teacher, who frequently
was neither well educated nor sophisticated, that focused on having the students memorize multiplication
tables had little to offer in comparison.

Mitchell was not alone in holding these views. Her old friend and now summer neighbor in Vermont, Agnes Hocking, also stimulated by the educational needs of her own children and by dissatisfaction with existing public schools in Cambridge, Massachusetts, established Shady Hill School along similar lines in 1915. The Laboratory School at the University of Chicago, a direct descendant of the school Dewey created while a professor there, and the Francis W. Parker School, also in Chicago, developed comparable programs.

In 1921 when her eldest son, Jack, was seven years old and her youngest, Arnold, three, Lucy Sprague Mitchell published the *Here and Now Story Book*, a compilation of two- to seven-year-olds' stories and rhymes as well as an explanation of children's use of language at different ages. It was an immediate success, establishing her nationally as a leading "progressive educator" whose fundamental interest was in children and their development and who sought schooling that would capitalize on a child's interests and experiences. In Mitchell's case the message was not anti-intellectual, as her own children received plenty of intellectual stimulation and expectation in their family home, at the homes of their summer neighbors (the men almost entirely professors at leading American universities) in Greensboro, Vermont, and in their Greenwich Village community. But for other children without such stimuli in more prosaic environments, namely the majority of American youth, Mitchell's message minimized the significance of knowledge. Further, it spoke not at all of "virtue," which seemed old-fashioned, but rather of healthy social and psychological adjustment, which appeared the modern equivalent. Children taught in such a way, she believed, would assure a democratic and progressive society, her version of "virtue."

As the decades of the twenties, thirties, and forties passed, the Bureau of Educational Experiments encompassed many different activities, including a nursery school, a teacher-training program, and an elementary school. Ultimately it became Bank Street College of Education, initially named for its location in Greenwich Village, but now established on the Upper West Side of Manhattan near Columbia University. During the 1940s, Mitchell and her colleagues finally found favor with the New York City public school system, which by then had moved to embrace much of the adjustment ethos, evidence of the spread of the shifting emphasis in schooling. Its administrators invited them to provide workshops for elementary teachers that would facilitate implementation of the new, more flexible curriculum mandated by the board of education.

Lucy Sprague Mitchell's career encapsulates the adjustment era. Having begun her work as an educator in the second decade of the century, she remained active professionally through the 1950s and continued writing (though not publishing much) until her death in 1967. Her work focused upon the children themselves: she sought their fulfillment as individuals, preferably as successful professionals like their parents, but she had no clear means of assuring their fulfillment. She was not systematic and in that regard, above all else, she typified the leaders of the adjustment era.

In addition to being unsystematic, she was typical of the educational leaders of this period in three ways. First, she was a woman, and most of the pioneers in the movement to create new schools were women, educated and, often, affluent women. Like that of her female colleagues, her work in New York City centered on children whose families provided many conventional educational advantages and for whom school was a supplement, not a principal provider of knowledge and virtue. Second, as an educator she felt both entitled and empowered to determine the kind of schooling a child should receive. She did not look to an outside public to determine what should be done in her school or with her children. Finally, her emphasis was upon the child and upon helping the child adjust to life. That was why she wanted "the child-centered school," a term that captured the motif of the adjustment era. The nation's need for an educated citizenry was not her primary concern though she believed it would be a subsidiary benefit of the kind of schooling she championed.

Not everyone was as enthusiastic about the "child-centered school" as the progressive educator colleagues of Lucy Sprague Mitchell were. One of her neighbors in Greenwich Village, not one of the bohemian elite but an Italian immigrant mother, commented to sociologist Caroline Ware about one of these schools (Elisabeth Irwin's Little Red School House where Mitchell had also taught):

> The program of that school is suited to the children of well-to-do homes, not to our children. We send our children to school for what we cannot give them ourselves, grammar and drill. The Fifth Avenue children learn to speak well in their homes. We do not send our children to school for group activity; they get plenty of that in the street. But the Fifth Avenue children are lonely, I can see how group experiences is an important form of education to them.

The wise Italian mother was right; families traditionally have asked schools to give what they could not give themselves.

CHILD-CENTERED SCHOOLS

The term of derision against which reformers in the 1920s, 1930s, and 1940s fought was "academic lockstep," by which they meant the "order" that their administrative predecessors had brought to the chaos of hordes of youngsters entering schools, many without facility in English. What the reformers sought was a "child-centered school" in which a child could comfortably adjust to life. John Dewey and his daughter, Evelyn, described the first of these schools in their 1915 book, *Schools of To-Morrow*. "To-Morrow" was slow to arrive in the schools of the United States, as are most educational reform movements, but twenty-five years later most American schools included some elements of child-centeredness. Forty years later "academic lockstep" was gone, much to the consternation of the public critics of that time.

If lockstep was the enemy, its primary embodiment became school furniture. Whether the student desks were movable or not became the visual signal of whether the school was rigid and bureaucratic or flexible and responsive. The old rows of school desks, bolted to the floor, one following behind the other—so convenient for dipping the pigtail of the girl in front of you into your built-in ink well—were to be replaced by individual chairs and little tables that students and teacher could rearrange at will. My own Indiana elementary school located in a college town, West Lafayette, had chairs and tables in the primary grades when I entered in 1940 but bolted desks in the later elementary grades. Elsewhere in southern Indiana and even in Marion County, site of the state capital, bolted desks persisted in the primary grades through the 1930s, gradually shifting during the following decade. Affluent suburban Chicago schools also had bolted primary desks in the mid-thirties. When I began teaching in 1955 in the Dismal Swamp in Virginia and later in Norfolk and New York City, I encountered only movable desks. As the desks moved, slowly, so did the curriculum and pedagogy.

The degree to which the schools achieved the essence of the reform or merely a poor imitation of it, however, became the basis of the controversies that confronted the educators of the 1950s. It was easier to replace bolted desks with movable furniture than it was, for example, to transform history teachers with a commitment to chronology into social studies teachers with a knowledge of the various social sciences and the pedagogical imagination to transform that knowledge into a means of helping their students explore their communities.

Curriculum, pedagogy, and school organization were all up for revision in the adjustment era. Small schools and elementary schools, which many of the new private schools were, had an immense organizational advantage that the large publics lacked. Schools with enrollments of seventy-five to one hundred and with pupils ranging in age from six to fourteen were better suited to individualizing instruction, grouping children according to their interests or skills, and generally avoiding the regulations deemed necessary when seven hundred or a thousand youngsters were herded into a single school building. The academic needs of elementary school students were basic: reading, arithmetic, a little writing, and, most of all, developing an interest in learning. High school and college preparatory curricula, which assumed knowledge of some subjects in some depth, presented much deeper challenges than did elementary schools, where the adjustment curriculum initially flourished.

If what children were supposed to know could be modified to fit their interests, then so too could changes be made in how they were supposed to act. Punctuality, neatness, beautiful and legible handwriting all declined as sought-after "virtues" in favor of creativity, spontaneity, and self-expression. Cursive writing became a lost art. Honesty and teamwork remained part of the pantheon of virtues.

Many "modern" parents, of course, loved the idea that their child's schoolwork was tailored to him or her. So did the new teachers drawn to these kinds of schools. Their instruction fell on much more receptive ears when it accorded with the youngsters' interests. These teachers also were free to design much more imaginative lessons than their colleagues in the city schools, where written, formal daily lesson plans for teachers were de rigueur. Many of these new teachers came not from normal schools or teachers colleges (primarily public institutions of low cost, low admissions standards, and, not surprisingly, low status) but rather from liberal arts colleges or universities and had much more sophisticated backgrounds than did the conventional public school teachers.

Finally, the curriculum expanded, not typically with the vocational studies that were entering the public schools, but rather with more imaginative reconstructions of the traditional disciplines and the arts. From these reorganizations came the disappearance of history and government as separate subjects and the emergence of "social studies," which was intended to integrate past and present human behavior. Ultimately social studies would merge with English to become "core subjects" intended to provide children with a unified approach to human experience. The traditional disciplines were thought to be artificial and narrow constructs and thus limiting and "unnatural." Children would benefit more from direct experience, progressive educators argued, and thus the curriculum would include trips to the local fire station, rather than a lesson about the history of devastating fires in Italy. Further, the new curriculum included extensive involvement with making art works, performing musical events, and even constructing models of past civilizations. For these children school became a place where you did not just learn passively from books and oral recitation but rather you created objects, reports, and "projects" with various constituent elements. Thus did John Dewey's expression "learning by doing" find life in these small schools beginning in the 1920s and becoming reasonably widespread in suburban and urban districts in the next two decades until even the behemoth New York City attempted to adopt such practices a quarter century later. As historian Diane Ravitch observes in *Left Behind*, "By the end of World War II, progressivism was the reigning ideology of American education."

At their best, these schools were the finest you could imagine for children, as Thomas S. Kuhn recalled. For the linguistically talented, reading and learning in the traditional manner were always available. But, for children who were not linguistically talented the new curriculum and pedagogy provided marvelous opportunities. If you could demonstrate your knowledge of ancient Rome by building a model of the Colosseum, instead of writing a term paper on its history, you could fulfill your requirements without relying solely on your linguistic skills. Many students found this form of compliance with academic demands much more to their liking than traditional tests, which receded in importance as indicators of subject matter mastery as the commitment to "projects," particularly ones involving a group, grew. Thus the pupils' "adjustment" was easier as they were not pushed to engage in activities they did not like. Traditionalists, however, wondered what the child had actually learned about Roman history.

For the children of privilege who attended them, these schools were a magnificent supplement to the rich educational environment of their homes and communities, as the Italian mother in Greenwich Village had observed. These were the sons and daughters of the professional and managerial classes who mostly lived in urban and the new suburban communities where success as adults came to the well educated, where public libraries with special sections for children's books were widely available, and where the community norm and expectation was college for all at a time when less than 10 percent of their age group were college students. Though schooling for these children was supplemental to their many and varied other educational influences, their parents vigorously insisted on the very best schools, thus insuring that these youngsters would have every possible advantage in their preparation for adult life. Their experiences in school fit into a niche in their overall educational program and were congruent with other experiences in their life, just as John Dewey had urged they be.

While school was an important but not determining educational experience for these children, the limited part that schooling played in their overall education was not widely recognized at the time. Certainly educators serving in the most admired school districts in the country were not likely to emphasize that schooling was not as important for their students, who had rich familial and community resources at their disposal, as it was for children without such advantages. Such school men understandably wanted to claim full credit for the success of their students whether the children learned the material in school or at home. Today, when we are more attuned to the influence that family and community experiences have in developing a child's sense of self, of opportunities, and of awareness of the world, it is easier to recognize that the schooling provided to these children was supplemental. Such was not the case for the majority of American youth in the 1920s who did not live in such educationally rich environments and for whom school was a primary, not supplemental, educational experience.

PUBLIC SCHOOL ADVOCATE OF ADJUSTMENT: CARLETON WASHBURNE

As Lucy Sprague Mitchell represented the early private school leaders in the adjustment era, so Carleton

Washburne exemplified the new public school educator of this period. Also born in Chicago but a decade later to a physician father and a mother active in educational and political affairs, Washburne too went west as a young person, initially intending to follow the profession of his father and grandfather, medicine. Washburne shared many qualities with most of the later leaders of the adjustment era, but differed from the early leaders, such as Mitchell. A white male with a strong but nonsectarian Protestant religious heritage, Midwestern in origin, liberal in social views, a practitioner turned professor of education, committed to the centrality of children and their social needs in the educational process, Washburne came from a well-educated but not wealthy family. Although Washburne was himself academically well trained at Stanford—and later earned a doctorate in the new field of "education" from Berkeley—he harbored a skepticism about the need for such formal learning in others.

Washburne failed in his first job, in business, and unlike Mitchell, his family could not support him financially. Consequently, he took the only position he could find and became a teacher of thirty-five students in grades four through eight in the rural, low-income La Puente district of Los Angeles County. Having no preparation for this assignment, Washburne relied heavily on what he recalled of his experience attending the Francis W. Parker School and his mother's work with Parker and her friendship with John Dewey. With little supervision and therefore freedom to experiment, Washburne reported that he utilized Parker's and Dewey's ideas to create a school garden, dramatizations, a school library, sex education, and "provision for adapting to individual differences."

By 1914 he convinced Frederic Burk, president of San Francisco State Normal School and author of *Lockstep Schooling and a Remedy*, to hire him for the faculty, where he remained for five years, while simultaneously earning a doctorate in education from the University of California, Berkeley. Burk was asked to recommend someone who shared his ideas for a superintendent position in a wealthy Chicago suburb, and, according to Washburne, he told him, "You are a very young man and Winnetka is a very small place; so if you fail it won't make a very big splash. I guess I'll recommend you."

The twenty-nine-year-old Washburne arrived in Winnetka as superintendent in 1919 and did not fail. He remained until 1943, by which time Winnetka was among the best-known school systems in the nation, largely because of Washburne's leadership. One enormous advantage for Washburne was that the district was limited to elementary schools, in which the reforms he initiated were much easier to implement than they would have been in a district in which high school students were included as well. Inevitably, parents of high school students in such communities insist that their children be well (and conventionally) prepared for the best colleges.

Washburne's twenty-four-year tenure at Winnetka was the pinnacle of his career, as he and his colleagues created a school system that many believed was one of the best in the nation. Following the principles that Burk, Parker, and Dewey had espoused, the community was deeply committed to providing the best possible education for its children, abhorring rigidity and seeking modernity. For them modernity meant individualized instruction for the children, who moved through the curriculum at their own paces and were supported by an able faculty to succeed in academically challenging work. Because the district did not include a high school, Winnetka was spared the necessity of determining what courses were necessary for college admission and completion. Successful and well-educated families that provided their healthy children with strong support for learning enabled the school to develop imaginative programs that served these youngsters well. The central idea that Washburne and the gifted colleagues whom he hired introduced was a method of individualizing instruction for classes of thirty or forty students by means of a novelty at the time, workbooks, which allowed elementary students to progress at their own rates. This innovation of individualized instruction evolved into broader projects and all subjects.

Winnetka parents formed a marvelously supportive community for their elementary schools. With the schools' innovative teachers, individualization meant helping each child complete the work in the time and manner appropriate for him or her. In less hospitable circumstances, namely most other communities, workbooks became a way of keeping pupils busy, and neither completion nor mastery of the material was assured. Washburne also pioneered cooperation with the nearby private schools—North Shore Country Day and his alma mater, Francis W. Parker School—in sharing facilities and training teachers in the new approach to education. The Graduate Teachers College of Winnetka explicitly sought graduates of liberal arts colleges with interests in children and prepared them for teaching, much as Mitchell's Bank Street College of Education did.

The general sense of freedom and creativity in Winnetka extended to Washburne himself. He explained his experience in Winnetka, which included several highly unusual paid leaves during the school year while he and his wife traveled abroad to learn about education,

> My wide range of interests seems to conflict with my professional career, but I managed to integrate most of them with it or to squeeze them into my non-professional life. . . . My civic interests, with my strongly liberal bent did cause

some conflict with the politically conservative community of Winnetka, in which I worked so many years. But I weathered the storms by the backing of those who felt that what I was doing for the schools was right and who respected my fiscal skill and administrative capacity.

Like Mitchell, Washburne benefited from the culturally enriching and intellectually broadening experiences of foreign travel and observations of divergent school arrangements, though, unlike Mitchell, Washburne found the funds through his paid leaves to finance himself, a talent that he needed as a public school administrator and that Mitchell, who had independent family inheritances, certainly lacked.

Washburne was effective in Winnetka, but for administrators in less hospitable environments and without his fiscal and managerial skills the task was more difficult. Creating child-centered schools meant understanding the interests and competencies of the child. Many who sent their children to such places believed that their sons and daughters were "gifted," a term that replaced "bright" in the current lexicon and was meant to imply a broader range of skills than simply the linguistic and logical ones. Both Mitchell and Washburne dealt with many families who considered their children to be considerably above average, if not "gifted."

TERMAN AND THE TRIUMPH OF TESTING

Soon the burgeoning mental testing movement would buttress families' claims that their children were gifted. Psychologist Lewis Terman—a professor of education at Stanford, one of the fathers of the Army Alpha, and, like Washburne, a white, male, Midwesterner of

Protestant origins—led the effort. Standardized testing, Terman claimed, had a scientific and, therefore, presumably accurate, means of identifying smart children.

Following World War I, Terman turned his attention from using the tests either for assessing the "feeble-minded," as they had originated under Alfred Binet in France, or for classification of Army personnel, as in the development of the Army Alpha, to identification of the gifted. This new purpose was more in keeping with the individualistic and developmentally focused ethos of the time. Beginning with teacher recommendations for the brightest and youngest students in their classes, Terman screened these nominees with a group intelligence test, and the highest scorers were then given the individual Stanford-Binet test, which yielded an IQ score. Those scoring IQs greater than 140 became subjects in his *Genetic Studies of Genius*. Among these students Russian Jews were over-represented and Italian Catholics underrepresented, thus triggering the nature versus nurture debates about intelligence that are with us still.

Soon the IQ became a standard measure in schools that were wealthy enough for all children to receive the Stanford-Binet test, which a trained psychologist had to administer individually (an expensive endeavor for a large school system). Adaptations of the Stanford-Binet, particularly the Otis tests, soon appeared. These were given to groups of children under pressures of time (many children did not have time to finish the test and hence received lower scores than the children who were quicker) and scored mechanically, a much less expensive means of getting an IQ score for a child. These group tests suffered even more than the individual tests did from concerns about validity and reliability, depending as they inevitably did first and foremost on the children's skill in reading and on the speed with which they answered questions.

Terman captured the spirit of the times when he spoke to the National Education Association in 1923 and characterized as a primary failure of the schools their inattention to the needs of gifted children. As Terman expressed it, "the typical gifted child *has already mastered the subject-matter 35 per cent beyond the norm for his age* [italics in original]." Since accelerating such children (skipping them ahead a grade) only moved them 14 percent above the norm for their age, Terman concluded, "the typical gifted child is being held 21 percent of his age below the level to which he has already mastered his work. I think this is a rather momentous fact." Such apparent precision in Terman's estimates gave the appearance that he was accurate in describing this phenomenon.

More than half of Terman's 140-IQ-plus children came from families in the top 4 or 5 percent of the "vocational hierarchy" (as was typical of the pupils in Mitchell's and Washburne's schools), and 80 percent came from the professional and semiprofessional classes. Terman, however, did not believe this finding challenged his conviction that the IQ test measured innate intelligence. Similarly, he determined that the "racial stocks" of the most gifted children were northern and western European (similar to his own Protestant Hoosier origins, incidentally) and Jewish, and he was concerned that these groups had much lower birth rates than the "Mediterranean, Mexican, and Negroes," few of whose children he identified as gifted.

Terman concluded his 1923 address with a forceful call to the educators to provide

> *differentiation of curriculum and of methods* such as will give to every child the type of educational diet from which he can derive the maximum nourishment. . . . The abandonment of the single-track, pre-high-school curriculum is in fact the first necessary step toward educational democracy. The single-track is a straight jacket which dwarfs

the mental development of the inferior as well as the gifted [italics in original].

This is guidance for adjustment with a vengeance and is based on the pretext that Terman's testing technology adequately indicated the youngsters' abilities, preferences, and temperaments—a dubious assumption.

The simplest way to understand and to implement Terman's message, and simplicity in both understanding and implementation was a hallmark of twentieth-century American educators, was to individualize instruction in keeping with children's abilities and interests. The notion that there was a core body of knowledge that all children should master, the idea advanced by Charles William Eliot and his Committee of Ten in 1893 for high school students and by eighteenth- and nineteenth-century textbook authors such as Noah Webster and William McGuffey, was vanishing rapidly. Pushing spelling, punctuation, number facts, multiplication tables, and tales of American heroism and high morality into the heads of reluctant learners had characterized the curriculum of assimilation, a sentiment now in rapid retreat and criticized for its "lockstep" nature.

One reason for the rapid decline in support for the old curriculum was both the emerging conviction and the reality that youngsters should spend more of their childhood in school. They were doing so, as the rising enrollments in high schools demonstrated. Clearly a formalistic, academic curriculum would not work year in and year out with children who had not learned the basics, and, therefore, had no skills to master advanced material, and who previously would have dropped out of school after the third or fourth grade. Students who had not understood addition, subtraction, and fractions would not be able to handle algebra.

Urban, industrial societies required more skills of workers than did rural ones, where housework, farming, and other jobs could be learned informally. Child labor legislation, passed in the early years of the century but only gradually enforced in the 1920s and 1930s, also increased the likelihood that children would remain in school longer. The lack of jobs during the Great Depression led to particularly escalated high school enrollments. These forces kept youngsters in school, but without changes in the pedagogy, there was little likelihood that they would prosper academically. The adjustment era promised through the child-centered school dramatic changes both in pedagogy and in curriculum. The pedagogical changes undoubtedly were beneficial in enhancing learning, but the conclusion that curriculum was flexible, that all subjects were of equivalent value, pretending that "general arithmetic" was as valuable as algebra, shortchanged dramatically the youngsters consigned to such subjects as "general arithmetic." That was not beneficial either to the children or to the nation.

Lengthening both the number of days in the school year and the number of years that a child was expected to spend in school, as well as encouraging more regular attendance, occurred simultaneously with these changes in the curriculum. Many believed that it would simply be impossible to keep previously unschooled pupils in school longer if the old curriculum remained in force. By 1920 almost 17 percent of the seventeen-year-olds were high school graduates and rising rapidly, reaching 60 percent in 1954.

Certainly it was easier to hold the reluctant learner in school if you did not worry about his mastering a subject at the level appropriate for his grade. Similarly it was more interesting for both student and teacher if the content of the class was based on mutual interests, not on some dull curriculum prepared by the state department of education. Thus, individualized instruction and a renunciation of traditional curriculum became the hallmarks of the child-centered school. By adopting these features, educators "adjusted" the school to the child, thereby helping the child adjust to life. And it was certainly handy for those educators who still recalled that public schools were supposed to serve democracy to be assured by the famous Stanford psychologist Lewis Terman that this was "the first necessary step toward educational democracy."

SEVEN CARDINAL PRINCIPLES AND THEIR LEGACY

Not only Terman but also the federal government through its Office of Education gave legitimacy to this modification of the school program. In 1918, just as World War I was ending, it published a National Education Association report by its Commission on the Reorganization of Secondary Education entitled *Cardinal Principles of Secondary Education*. This document, born of the rising number of children in high school in the first two decades of the century, reified the idea that high school was about something other than mastery of academic material. Only one of the seven principles mentioned academic matters at all, "command of the fundamental processes," which one might have thought was a principle of elementary, not secondary, education.

These seven principles, which remained a staple of professional education for future teachers well into the second half of the twentieth century, stressed non-academic goals for the high school. They captured the tension between the American ideals of virtue and knowledge as the twin goals of education. In addition to the "fundamental processes" goal, the other six were health, worthy home membership, vocation, civic education, worthy use of leisure time, and ethical character. These were to form the high school curriculum of adjustment, which persisted for many years until the renewed testing and "standards" movement arose near the end of the century.

The seven goals attracted such a favorable reaction that in 1927 the National Congress of Parents and Teachers (whose president that year was a Winnetka woman, Mrs. B. F. Langworthy) included them in its fundamental platform and concluded that it had "becoming increasingly apparent that these [cardinal principles] are the objectives not only of the high school, but of all education." Perhaps therein lay the difficulty. As goals for growing up, the principles seem quite reasonable, but as goals for schooling, a more specialized function than simply "growing up," they lack the focus on academic learning that schools might be expected to undertake as their principal contribution to a child's development. This was the adjustment dilemma: did schools have a unique obligation to help children learn academic material or did they simply help a child adjust to life? For most of the middle years of the twentieth century the schools' special responsibility for teaching academic subjects to all children was minimized. The lines between a child's learning and a child's development, particularly for those children for whom not much was expected academically, were murky. Typically development triumphed over learning in the agenda of many schools.

With Mitchell and Washburne arguing that the school should be "child-centered," with Terman justifying separate programs for the gifted and the nongifted, and the National Education Association and federal government alleging that the goals for high school education were primarily nonacademic, the schools were left quite free to modify their programs in ways that would fit their perception of their students' needs and help them "adjust to life." In short, elementary teachers in the 1920s were able to follow Charles William Eliot's advice to "sort their children by their evident or probable destiny" and secondary teachers now had both the technology to do so (Terman's tests) and the philosophical rationale to legitimize such revised curriculum (the Seven Cardinal Principles). Everyone should have been satisfied, but they were not.

JOURNALISTS CRITIQUE THE EDUCATORS

Like the reporters who drew attention to the urban, immigrant populations in the nineteenth century, journalists again led the way in criticizing school practices. One of the most influential journalists of the twentieth century, Walter Lippmann, challenged the testers. Having completed his bachelor's degree at Harvard in three years, done graduate work, and served in the army in World War I, where presumably he encountered the Army Alpha, Lippmann like Terman came from one of the "racial stocks" that did best on the standardized tests; he was Jewish. At age thirty-three he was associate editor of the liberal journal *New Republic*, for which he wrote a devastating series of articles in 1922 challenging the claims of the leaders of the testing movement that they, in fact, were measuring innate intelligence. Lippmann described the intelligence test as "an instrument for classifying a group of people, rather than a 'measure of intelligence.'" Classification was precisely why school people were using the tests, but with the rationale that the classification was on the basis of intelligence and thereby justified. Lippmann said "no" both to the claim that the tests measured intelligence and to the claim that Terman and his colleagues knew what intelligence was.

While Terman concentrated upon the value of the tests in identifying the gifted and providing special programs for them, Lippmann, particularly, warned about the misuse of tests in classifying children as backward. As he stressed in his articles, "the danger of the intelligence tests is that in a wholesale system of education, the less sophisticated or the more prejudiced will stop when they have classified and forget that their duty is to educate. They will grade the retarded child instead of fighting the causes of his backwardness." Lippmann further argued that

> [Testers] believe they are measuring the capacity of a human being for all time and that this capacity is fatally fixed by the child's heredity. . . . If the intelligence test really measured the unchangeable heredity capacity of human beings, as so many assert, it would inevitably evolve from an administrative convenience into a basis for hereditary caste.

NEW CURRICULUM FOR THE MASSES

Faced with rapidly growing enrollments, school leaders certainly sought administrative convenience, particularly when justified by men of science, as the testers claimed to be. The results of testing favored the children of high status Americans, the group most likely to complain if things were not going well for their children. These parents generally rejoiced while their children encountered talented and caring teachers in settings that were pleasant and incorporated the arts and other stimuli into renovated buildings and reorganized curricula. What could be better?

For the bulk of the enrollment, however, the changes were less favorable. Particularly as the nation sank into the depression of the 1930s, many children of the working class were unable to find immediate employment and remained in school much longer as the high school graduation figures illustrate. In 1930, 29 percent of seventeen-year-olds were high school graduates, while the percentage jumped to more than 50 in 1940.

Most of these new high school attendees did not meet Terman's definition of "gifted," and their curriculum and pedagogy were determined by the Seven Cardinal Principles, which were intended to help them adjust to what would be their adult lives. Since there was no consensus on a common high school curriculum that would be valuable for all, courses that had been considered traditional and required, such as algebra, geometry, European history, foreign languages, chemistry, physics, as well as four years of English, were frequently dropped or made optional. Replacements for material taught in English classes exemplify this: English classics such as *Silas Marner* or Shakespeare's plays were exchanged for "easier" material. Even this new material, such as the novels of Pearl Buck, seemed too demanding. Soon English itself was dropped as a requirement and replaced with "journalism," "speech," and ultimately "language arts" and "communication" classes, all in the name of modernity and meeting the child's needs.

Vocational courses expanded widely, particularly for those for whom high school was seen as terminal education. These were, of course, the majority of high school students. Extracurricular activities expanded rapidly, from student government (deemed an "exercise in democracy") to sports (a venue for sportsmanship and teamwork) to arts and drama programs (opportunities for creativity) to student newspapers (a forum for writing skills combined with ethical principles of reporting and editing). All of these emphasized the virtue part of the curriculum; knowledge seemed important only for a few.

PROFESSORS SHAPE EDUCATIONAL PRIORITIES

As the depression took hold, Americans following discussions about education increasingly heard education professors, particularly at Teachers College, Columbia, calling teachers to arms in the fight for economic and social reform. Teachers College was the undisputed leader of institutions preparing teachers and school administrators both in regular courses and in enormous summer programs.

George S. Counts, a Kansan educated at the University of Chicago and a faculty member at Teachers College since 1927, spoke and wrote calling upon the schools to be "progressive," a term that now carried a leftist political intent as well as an educational one. In his best-known pamphlet, "Dare the School Build a New Social Order?" (1932), Counts urged the public schools to lead in developing an American society that was more socially just than the capitalistic government that had brought on the depression. Like his colleague across 120th Street at Columbia, John Dewey, Counts and his friend Carleton Washburne had also traveled to the Soviet Union in 1929 as part of a delegation hosted by the Russian trade unions. He chronicled his experiences and his enthusiasms in *A Ford Crosses Russia* (1930) and, like Dewey, initially found much there to admire, educationally and socially.

Meanwhile, the American public was leaving education to the educators while they dealt with issues of more immediate importance to themselves, such as finding a job or keeping one. The *New Republic*, faithful chronicler of educational activities throughout the first half of the century, gave George S. Counts space to explain his views as one of the newly recognized educational spokesmen in America. In 1932, he advised its liberal readers,

The weakness of progressive education thus lies in the fact that it has elaborated no theory of social welfare, but reflecting the point of view of the members of the liberal-minded upper-middle-class who send their children to the progressive schools—persons who are fairly well off, who have abandoned the faiths of their fathers, who assume an agnostic attitude toward all important questions. . . . If progressive education is to be genuinely progressive, it must emancipate itself from the influence of this class, face squarely and courageously every social issue . . . and become less frightened than it is today of the bogies of *imposition* and *indoctrination* . . . in a word, progressive education cannot place its trust in a child-centered school.

The manifestos of Counts and his colleagues dominated the prescriptive literature for education in the 1930s and certainly caught the attention of some professional educators, primarily professors of education and a few teachers and administrators. These debates, however, never gripped the mass of teachers or administrators nor did they attract broad interest from the American public or its government. What they did do, however, was to broaden the schooling debates, reminding teachers and the public that schooling had a civic dimension, one that was nearly obliterated by the debates about adjustment.

Teachers and school administrators meanwhile were busy trying to figure out how to provide programs that would keep children in school, particularly at a time of high unemployment. Easing the academic nature of the courses to "adjust" to students' perceived interests now had some legitimacy. This was the legacy of the child-centered school. While these debates were going on, the federal government was creating the Social Security system for all Americans, establishing the National Youth Administration to deal with out-of-school adolescents, the Civilian Conservation Corps to provide jobs for non-college-bound youth, and continuing de jure segregation by race in southern schools. In New York City, the community of the Teachers College faculty, an estimated fifteen thousand teachers were out of work. None of these issues attracted much attention from the professors of education.

The professors persisted, however, in developing new publications to advance their views. *The Educational Frontier,* edited by William Heard Kilpatrick in 1933 and including contributions from several of his Teachers College colleagues, placed educational issues in the social context of the day. Later many of these authors contributed to the new journal *The Social Frontier*, which began publication in 1935. Historian Raymond Callahan in *Education and the Cult of Efficiency* praised it as "a journal which in its short life was the most outstanding and courageous journal American education has produced." Others, however, observed that discussions of Marxism, class struggle, and the teachers' role in helping children understand these matters—some called it indoctrination—did not play well with the broad American public. Although Americans were concerned about the problems of the depression, on the whole, they were not willing to accept radical solutions to their troubles.

Perhaps unintentionally, these professors poignantly illustrated the gap between theory and practice in education, which Dewey had repeatedly deplored, and the reluctance of school people to change their local practice instantly in accordance with new views espoused by distant experts. Many American intellectuals were critical of their government after the excesses of the 1920s and the visible suffering of so many of their countrymen in the 1930s. Counts and many of his colleagues at Teachers College were outspoken in their condemnation of governmental inadequacies. Secure in tenured positions at a prospering institution, they called upon their practitioner colleagues to assert their criticisms of the government in the schools. Not surprisingly, school superintendents in wealthy suburbs, who formed an important leadership cadre of American schooling, were reluctant to follow their advice. Carleton Washburne in Winnetka, particularly, tried to soften Counts's critique. Dependent as these superintendents were upon school boards who hired (and fired) them, they generally avoided the fiery rhetoric of the education professors and kept their attention upon the local community issues of helping their students "adjust to life." Their answer to Counts's question of whether the schools dared to build a new social order was "no."

By the end of the 1930s, and after knowledge of the purges the government of the Soviet Union conducted against its citizens spread, Dewey, Counts, and other leading spokesmen on education modified their rhetoric to stress the role of American schools in fostering democracy, a theme that had been of interest to Dewey since he began writing about education in the 1890s. By 1939 even the *Wall Street Journal* was praising Counts and Teachers College for the "conspicuous success" of its Congress on Education for Citizenship in Democracy. Despite a "surface tone of differing views," the *Journal* reported "something approaching unanimity" on the proposition that "Democracy . . . was much more than a mere political structure or an outward form; that it was a 'way of life,' the 'American way of life.' . . . this way of life rested at bottom on the concept of human *personality* [italics in original] as the thing for which 'Democracy' exists."

Defining democracy as a "way of life" rooted in "personality," rather than a system of political organization dependent upon informed and free participation by citizens in selecting the leaders of their government, obfuscated its relationship to schooling. One would have thought that the school system's obligation in a democracy was to ensure that all young people developed the knowledge and virtue that would enable them to become responsible adult citizens. Undoubtedly the ambiguity and abstraction of the Teachers College conference's statement eased its acceptance among the educators. "Personality" was a category that the adjustment folks took seriously as a modern concept. "Democracy" was a popular and familiar term, but one without much concrete meaning for education, particularly at a time when democracy was emerging from profound criticism and the United States was about to join forces in World War II with European allies, including Soviet Russia after the dissolution of the Nazi-Soviet pact.

Most educational practitioners (schoolteachers and administrators), however, were still worrying in the 1930s about avoiding the academic lockstep that had characterized their institutions in the early years of the century and still influenced many of them. Such rigidities clearly damaged the "personalities" of many children though their relationship to "democracy" was less clear. Many schools had not even reached the stage that Counts was arguing they should move beyond, the child-centered school. Further, their curriculum discussions were either about vocational education courses and who should take them or about integrating instruction in the humanities and social sciences. The growing acceptance of the anti-intellectual Seven Cardinal Principles gave school men license essentially to do whatever they wanted in the curriculum. Intelligence testing was becoming widespread, and the results of these tests gave the teachers legitimacy in making decisions about which children should take which subjects.

While the professors proclaimed, other educators were seeking money from foundations, particularly the Rockefeller family's General Education Board and the

In contrast to instructors at the progressive schools serving the affluent, Miss Pruss (fourth row, far left) focused on teaching reading to her forty-three white first-graders at the Springfield School in Raymond, Indiana, 1939. The constituency of this southern Indiana school attended by my husband, Loren Graham (third row, far right), was not affluent, as evidenced by the barefoot children in the front row.
Courtesy of Loren R. Graham

Carnegie Corporation, to support research that would justify the curricular and pedagogical practices embraced by the type of upper-middle-class school Counts had associated with progressive education. The most important of these studies was the Thirty School Study, also called the Eight Year Study, which traced the collegiate experiences of the graduates of these high schools, which in the end comprised eighteen public and sixteen private institutions. Wilford Aikin, then head of the John Burroughs School in St. Louis and subsequently, like so many of his progressive educator colleagues, on the education faculty of Ohio State University, led the commission and found to no one's surprise, but to the immense relief of the researchers, that the graduates of the "progressive schools" did as well academically in selective colleges as the graduates of "traditional" schools. Spelling and ancient history turned out not to be necessary for success at Harvard; creative writing and social studies, whatever they involved, worked just as well, as Thomas Kuhn's "summa" illustrated. The rationale became "curriculum does not make a difference" if graduates of progressive schools who did not follow the traditional academic preparation did as well at Princeton or Yale as alumni of more traditional private schools such as St. Paul's or Groton.

The results of these studies justified in the minds of the progressive educators the value of their enterprise. More important, this study legitimized the practice increasingly found throughout American high schools of providing a different curriculum for various kinds of students: college-bound, vocational, and general track (everybody else). This was the ultimate form of adjustment in the child-centered school: deciding what the child should learn based on adult perceptions of the child's interests and abilities. The selection criteria were a mix of the immediately discernible characteristics (race and gender), with the easily recognizable ones (class), and the "scientific" ones (test scores, which were heavily influenced by race and class and to a lesser degree by gender).

The multivolume analysis of the Thirty School Study launched the field of educational evaluation, and the career of its principal author, Ralph Tyler. Tyler, like Washburne, Terman, Counts, and many of the other professors of education of this era, was a white man of Protestant origins reared in moderate circumstances in the Midwest who came to the study of education from several years of school teaching in relatively small communities. These men believed, based on their own life experience, that doing well in school was nearly all that was needed to be a success, because that had been true for them. Such was not the case, of course, for women, for racial minorities, for Roman Catholics and Jews, for the majority of the U.S. population, all of whom were vastly underrepresented in the educational leadership of that era. This homogeneity of experience obscured for many of them the important role family and community played in learning, as well as the outright discrimination against persons who did not share their gender, race, or religion.

This cultural blindness underlay Tyler's evaluation of the Eight Year Study. One fundamental point failed to become salient: graduates of the "progressive" schools, such as Thomas Kuhn, were likely to have come from educationally rich homes and communities and for them school was simply an additional instructional course in their already rich academic and cultural diet. If they attended elementary schools such as Mitchell's Bank Street or Washburne's Winnetka, then they were likely to have well-prepared, committed teachers who helped them explore subjects that caught their fancy in imaginative ways in an ordered environment. Further, the selective and expensive colleges these graduates attended in the depression years of the 1930s attracted

---

Facing page *(top)* The contrast in educational opportunities between those enjoying the best of New York City's schools and African Americans in the segregated South was immense, as demonstrated by this 1941 classroom in Veazy, Greene County, Georgia, heated with a stove, and *(bottom)* this mother trying to help her children learn in Louisiana in 1939 despite her own poor grasp of grammar ("the rain are fallin"). *Library of Congress, Prints & Photographs Division, FSA-OWI Collection, [LC-USF34-046248-D], [LC-USF34-031938-D]*

almost entirely young people of similar backgrounds. Therefore, it was not the school curriculum but rather the family, home, and cultural experience that prepared students for college success. Not surprisingly, family, home, and culture were more important educationally than school by itself, a point that became increasingly clear to educational researchers in the second half of the twentieth century.

PUBLIC PERCEPTIONS OF SCHOOLS

Despite the professors' pronouncements and researchers' results, Americans in this period were not particularly concerned about the education of their youth. Such silence left the education professors free from criticism of their views. A January 1939 Gallup poll that asked, "What do you regard as the most important problem before the American people today?" found 39 percent listing unemployment and 10 percent, world peace. Sixteen other items drew at least 1 percent of respondents. "Training the youth," the response closest to education, was one of fifty additional items that included such topics as "married women in jobs" or "the use of leisure time" mentioned by less than 0.5 percent of the respondents. In 1941 only 1 percent of either men or women considered education a subject "most talked about" among their friends and acquaintances.

The professors of education persisted, however limited their following. The multivolume report of the Eight Year Study emerged in 1942 when Americans' attention was focused not on issues of curriculum or college but on winning World War II. Attention in schools focused upon what youngsters could do "to support the war effort." Nonetheless, with additional foundation support, the study spun off several additional commissions, the principal one led by V. T. Thayer, the head of the Ethical Culture Schools in New York City. Thayer's group looked at how the secondary school curriculum should be revised, and concluded "the chief task of secondary education to be that of helping adolescents to secure for themselves values, emotional unity, skill, understanding and purposefulness of life." This was the curriculum of adjustment.

As American and Allied military victories advanced both in Europe and in the Pacific, and ultimate victory began to appear likely, adjustment or readjustment issues assumed great significance. Still fresh in the memories of the middle-aged men who led these plans for peacetime and clear to their younger colleagues, the depression, which had essentially ended with American mobilization for World War II, remained a potential threat. When the soldiers, sailors, and the civilians who had worked in the war industries sought jobs in a nation at peace unemployment could, once again, become a national problem. The return of military men was a particularly pressing issue as most were young, and many had interrupted their schooling when they enlisted or were drafted. Others were young enough that they could plausibly go back to school, either to college or vocational or technical schools, for additional training and stay off the glutted job market for a few years until the economy could absorb them. From these concerns came the Servicemen's Readjustment Act of 1944, better known as the GI Bill.

LIFE ADJUSTMENT AS GOAL

If the colleges were expected to help in readjustment, then the high schools needed to assist in adjustment. Educators reactivated their interest in how secondary schools could foster adolescents' entry into adulthood. Gradually a new term entered the educational lexicon, "life adjustment." Its father, Charles Prosser—another white, male, midwestern educator, who had played a leading role in developing vocational education in the first decades of the century—introduced the term to a conference in 1945. Prosser successfully called on the U.S. Office of Education to establish a commission to study the matter. Benjamin Willis, then the superintendent in Yonkers, New York, and ultimately in Chicago, where his policies of providing better schools for whites than blacks brought him considerable notoriety, chaired the Commission on Life Adjustment Education for Youth.

Prosser's timing was exquisite, coming as it did as high school enrollments continued to increase while academic mastery among the students did not. His proposal argued that only 20 percent of American youth could benefit from an academic curriculum while another 20 percent would find a vocational curriculum useful and the balance (60 percent) should receive "life adjustment training." Life adjustment training became the curricular codification of the Seven Cardinal Principles, now broadly accepted more than thirty years after their initial enunciation. The commission accepted these sentiments and gave its principal attention to children's nonacademic needs, "physical, mental and emotional health . . . the present problems of youth as well as their preparation for future living . . . the importance of personal satisfactions and achievements for each individual within the limits of his abilities." In short, anything goes as curriculum in the high school, thereby reducing the academic legitimacy of a high school diploma though it would take several decades for that to become evident.

By 1952, Professor L. Thomas Hopkins of Teachers College urged his colleagues attending a national conference on life adjustment education, "We must take fear out of education. . . . Let us have a permissive environment, an informal releasing environment." At the same meeting Ralph Tyler, by then professor at the University of Chicago, anticipated the coming debates and argued that to achieve "equal educational opportunity for youth" it was essential to develop a course of studies that would "reach the intellectually gifted on the one hand and the mechanical-minded on the other." The same year New York's superintendent, William Jansen, issued his city's "six major goals of a sound public school education for America's youth." These goals were "adequate knowledge and skills, good social character for living in a democracy, good health, sound thinking, creative expression and appreciation, and adjustment to the world of work." This was the pabulum of virtue and knowledge for the midcentury, weak and tasteless and only moderately nourishing for some. These views gained wide adherence among the practitioners who were expected to organize their schools in accordance with these principles and also to find support for them in their communities. Initially these policies did just that, but the absence of attention to mastering traditional academic subjects became a serious problem, particularly as the teachers who had accepted that obligation as their principal task retired and were replaced by faculty without strong academic orientations.

Although one could find critics of the idea and practice of education for adjustment throughout the 1930s and 1940s, they did not become vociferous until the 1950s. Several reasons explain this delay. First, school enrollments were growing dramatically both as a consequence of the rising birth rate in the 1940s and the increasing belief that more schooling was valuable for adulthood. Some means of organizing the students, particularly the difficult adolescents, had to be found. The adjustment policy, which diminished the need for teachers to insure that all students learn academic material, previously considered the essence of the secondary school curriculum, allowed the inclusion of these recalcitrant scholars without unduly disturbing the institution.

Second, the principal voices in the discussion of what the schools should do were those of professors of education, a group which had come of age as a profession in the years following World War I, the adjustment era, and who, as noted earlier, were a remarkably homogeneous group. These professors and occasional superintendents and private school heads gave legitimacy to a renunciation of the academic curriculum as it had been known. Of course, most of them had received their own education through mastery of that curriculum, but many believed it was not necessary for others, in either its content or, certainly, in the lockstep pedagogy they had endured. In the best of their schools, with imaginative, effective teachers and lively students from homes committed to their education, the new arrangements worked well. Those were the schools and children that the professors saw at the Lincoln School at Teachers College or the Laboratory School at the University of Chicago or in the suburban communities of Palo Alto, Scarsdale, or Newton, where they made their homes. These professors' attention was typically not drawn to the schools of Compton, California; Harlem; South Boston; or rural Alabama. Obviously not all professors of education in the twenties, thirties, and forties held these views; William C. Bagley at Teachers College was a prominent exception. The new foundation funding, however, supported the efforts of the majority, and money, particularly for those unaccustomed to it, was a powerful stimulus.

Third, priorities other than education captured the attention of Americans during the Roaring Twenties, the depression of the thirties, and the war (hot and cold) of the forties. By the beginning of the fifties, as Americans settled into the prolonged ambiguity of the Cold War and the uncertain ways of winning it, noneducators again became interested in education. Concern about the nation and its capacity to solve important problems led some Americans to look for solutions in education. For many, education is seen as a means to an end, not as a good in itself. When the nation has faced an intractable social dilemma, education often has been used as a means to solve it. Neither the depression nor World War II seemed to most Americans solvable primarily through education. Even though some professors, such as George S. Counts, called upon education to change the social order during the depression, this was not a goal that was widely shared by the rest of the society, despite their dissatisfaction with the status quo. Invocation of the term "education for democracy," although frequently used, had little meaning in the broader society. It sounded good but did not mean much.

Public criticism regarding schooling began to build slowly after the U.S. victory in World War II, an effort that had dominated American public opinion from the late 1930s through the mid-1940s. At the opening of the school year in 1946, a Gallup poll reported that 87 percent of Americans were satisfied with the school their offspring attended. This result foreshadowed polling data that persisted through the last half of the twentieth century: parents liked their own children's school experiences better than they regarded the performance of American schools in general. Altering the curriculum to make it more immediately meaningful to students and adopting the policy of "social promotion" (moving a child through the grades whether he had learned the curriculum or not), basic elements of the adjustment agenda, were now being implemented in schools around the country. By 1954 nearly half the respondents to Gallup poll questions about schools' grouping of children based on the results of intelligence tests cited "psychological effects" (presumably negative) on children as a result of this practice. Despite its negative cast, this response illustrated the widespread acceptance of psychological factors as an influence on education, which had been a preeminent tenet of the early adjustment era.

By the beginning of the fifties, professors of education had largely driven themselves into isolation by retaining their commitment to the ideology of adjustment while public critics began to push other activities for the schools. These professors, now mostly at state university schools of education, particularly Illinois and Ohio State, as well as their old bastion, Teachers College, Columbia, no longer enjoyed a broad following nationally. Soon they would become objects of ridicule in the emerging educational protest literature as colleagues in the academic departments of their universities and other writers attacked them. Most of the teachers and administrators around the country, however, had studied at these institutions, and they took back to their professional work what their professors had taught them. Thus, the professors' latent influence was considerable even if their reputation was badly tarnished.

Both Lucy Sprague Mitchell and Carleton Washburne remained active educators in New York City in the 1950s, Mitchell as acting president and chair of the Board of Trustees at Bank Street College of Education and Washburne at Brooklyn College. Both were responsible for preparing educators, many of whom expected to find employment in local public schools. Both remained committed to their ideas of individualizing instruction and helping children develop fully, emotionally and socially. Bank Street continued to attract many academically strong candidates who wished to be elementary teachers, and at that time many of their graduates found employment in New York's best private and suburban public schools, where the clientele reflected Lucy Sprague Mitchell's friends and family.

On the other hand, Washburne, who had left Winnetka during World War II, became chairman of the department of education at Brooklyn College in 1949, when life adjustment was at its pinnacle. Now he was preparing schoolteachers and administrators not for suburban Winnetka, an environment he understood, but rather for Brooklyn, an environment in which he had no experience. His graduates were being hired to teach in neighborhoods that were home to some of the most troubling racial confrontations around schooling in the 1960s. One explanation for the frightful problems between teachers and the community members in the subsequent decades is that the values of adjustment, taught at Brooklyn College and other teacher preparation institutions, failed to prepare the teachers for their experiences in the Bedford-Stuyvesant and Ocean Hill–Brownsville classrooms in the 1960s. Children in those classes depended much more heavily on the school curriculum to learn academic material than did children in Winnetka, where alternative educational resources were rich. If a school failed to teach the child successfully in Brooklyn, and many did, the child had lost a prime chance in life. Those communities did not seek adjustment to the status quo for their children but rather access to better educational programs, and they hoped, as a result of them, for a better life for their children.

THREE

Access
1954–1983

"I'LL NEVER GO TO SCHOOL WITH A NIGGER!" Dickie, an eighth grader in my social studies class, shouted vehemently as we began to discuss the *Brown* v. *Board of Education* case prohibiting segregation in public schools that the Supreme Court had decided a year before, in 1954. Dickie was right; he never did, dropping out of school two years later, before his Virginia public high school began desegregation. I was flabbergasted and appalled by Dickie's assertion, only gradually coming to realize that my new profession, teaching, was heading on a rocky road to improvement.

In September 1955, as a new, navy bride, I began teaching in still segregated Deep Creek High School serving the predominantly low-income white community of the Dismal Swamp in southeastern Virginia. Prepared as I had been by the mushy adjustment curriculum of my Indiana public schools (lots of attention to my deficient social skills, not much to strengthening my intellect), I had zipped through college. I added the teacher training sequence after I became engaged in order to have a saleable skill when I married on graduation day. My five education courses, most of which I thought academically and professionally worthless, required that I memorize the Seven Cardinal Principles, still the reigning dogma, and I did, believing they represented the fuzzy thinking I associated with public education. I lived in a totally white world, never having had a black friend, fellow student, or teacher.

Under Virginia law at that time Deep Creek High School was also a totally white high school world, though surrounded by a black community. The drop-out rate was high: 140 students in eighth grade but only 40 high school seniors. When Dickie made his assertion about segregation, I was astounded both by the language and by the sentiment. We did not use such a term in my household, and, innocent that I was, I thought the Supreme Court had decided the year before in *Brown* v. *Board of Education* that public schools could not be legally segregated by race. I had not understood the political crafting of the phrase "all deliberate speed" in the 1955 *Brown* implementation decision, which delayed desegregation for decades.

As a beginning teacher in 1955, I found both the academic quality of the school and its racial attitudes appalling. I also learned that many of the children came from homes in which books, even newspapers, were not present, both because the families had little money and because many of the adults were not much interested in reading or did not read well themselves. Early on, I asked my eighth graders to bring an article from the newspaper to class the next day and learned to my astonishment that a number did not have newspapers in their homes. While most of the teachers did not use Dickie's language, many held similar views. Their own academic experience in small, local public and private colleges had limited the intellectual and cultural horizons of many of them, though my neighbor across the hall, Nell Casteen, was a powerful exception and a remarkable teacher.

When I left at the end of the year, terminated because I was pregnant, I remembered the students and some of my colleagues fondly. But I understood that American education was in serious trouble if the problems I encountered at Deep Creek—with its meager academic program for poor students, most of whom had few supplementary educational resources at home, and its unconstitutional racial attitudes—were widespread. I feared that Deep Creek was more typical than I had known, and I was right.

When I returned on Valentine's Day, 1991, to visit Deep Creek for the first time since my abrupt departure, I found an entirely different school though still located in the same building and community. The trophy cases, which had been nearly empty in 1955 (then only holding a third place track trophy from 1927), were now full, attesting to the academic, athletic, musical, and theatrical abilities of the students and their faculty advisors. The drop-out rate was sharply diminished. A strong academic curriculum prevailed, and a "warrant" was issued for all graduating seniors assuring potential employers of the student's competence and promise. A school orchestra had been created, and students played remarkably well both classical and popular music. Nathan Hardee, a local man who had been a sophomore when I taught there, has been principal since 1972.

"What accounts for all these improvements?" I asked. The story emerged from the photographs of the senior classes and principals hanging in the main corridor. I spotted my seniors, the class of 1956, like their predecessors, a small group of white students. Gradually the number of seniors increased, and by the sixties they began to include black students as well. As the number of blacks increased, the turnover of the principals increased, indicating the tumult that the school faced during the early years of desegregation. By the late 1970s the seniors were nearly equally divided by race, and the principals were no longer turning over nearly annually. The explanation, the administrators assured me, lay in the required desegregation, not welcomed by the whites in the community. The combination of federal requirements and funds both for desegregation and for additional instruction for low-income children as well as local leadership, both black and white, had brought Deep Creek a fine high school. Dickie would have been lucky to attend.

INADEQUACY OF ORDINARY SCHOOLING

My experience at Deep Creek illustrated three principal problems of American schooling in midcentury: racism, limited academic achievement for many students, and especially poor academic quality for the low-income students who needed good schooling most. Obviously those least served were low-income children of color, a group that most white educators had heretofore rarely considered.

The laissez faire approach of the adjustment era, 1920 to 1954, minimized the importance of traditional academic subjects, and many American youth did not bother much with them. Nor did the school men. This attitude of educators persisted through the fifties, sixties, and seventies, making ordinary schooling unsatisfactory for too many students. Few efforts to overhaul existing "regular schooling" emerged.

Rather, from the *Brown* decision in 1954 until the publication of *A Nation at Risk* in 1983, piecemeal solutions to these problems were sought without fundamentally addressing the need for school reform as a whole. These partial solutions for different constituencies make up the access era, in which public critics, federal officials, anxious parents, and baffled but determined school men attempted to provide a special program to fit the particular problem presented.

Access was intended both for the gifted and for the disenfranchised. The issue was getting into the program, and the energy was focused on access, not the quality of the program itself. The assumption, of course, was that the program to which one had gained access was preferable to the ordinary school program. Sometimes it was, sometimes not.

While the enthusiasm for access reflected widespread concern over the adequacy of ordinary schooling, the kind of access sought varied widely. Some wanted special programs offering academic enrichment to the "gifted and talented"; others sought a racially desegregated classroom. For others "access" meant having special additional instruction provided through the first major federal aid to education act, which was intended for schools with many students from low-income families. For still others it meant a curriculum adapted to the needs of non-English-speaking children. For others, it meant participation in a classroom with "normal" children rather than one limited to the "handicapped." For girls it involved support for sports and other programs equivalent to those available to boys.

These activities also brought together the roles of schooling in serving the needs of the children (the focus on adjustment) and the nation (the focus on assimilation). Both foci found expression in access. The stated rationale for programs for the "gifted and talented" was to benefit the children who were not being "challenged" with existing schoolwork and also the country, as it needed their skills to compete more effectively with the Soviet Union in the Cold War. Similarly segregation was perceived by the Supreme Court to be bad for black children, whose psyches suffered from it, and whose schools were dramatically inferior in resources to those of whites. It was also bad for the country insofar as it violated the constitutional principles enunciated in the Fourteenth Amendment of due process and equal protection of law. President Lyndon Johnson's Great Society legislation and his War on Poverty linked schooling issues to citizens' civil rights by promoting desegregation in schools and mandating changes in the manner in which schools served students with limited English, the handicapped, and girls. In short, the twin promises of knowledge and virtue could be sustained with the gifted augmenting their knowledge substantially and those participating in desegregation contributing to civic virtue. In general, the two worlds failed to come together immediately. Deep Creek took two decades to unite them.

SCHOOLS REGAIN PUBLIC ATTENTION

During the relatively quiescent period from 1920 to the early 1950s the public gave relatively little attention to education as other issues, the depression and World War II, dominated the news. Professional educators essentially had the schools to themselves. Educators lost their stage, however, when the American public found its voice as the Cold War evolved and as concerns about inequalities in American life expressed themselves in schooling. Two groups dominated the discussion and the action: public critics and federal officials. Though not nearly as well organized as the other two groups, parents sought "good schools," whatever that meant, for their growing families.

By 1954 no one seemed satisfied with education, and programs serving different interests proliferated. But the variety of programs led to a fragmentation of educational efforts. Even the phrase, "equality of educational opportunity," which was often used to characterize the period, failed to encompass the profoundly different school experiences encountered by students in "gifted and talented" classes and by those embroiled in confrontations over desegregation in which the safety of the students became more important than their mastery of mathematics. Regular programs continued with the weakened life adjustment curriculum. Unlike the previous thirty-five years, when the educators had explained to Americans what the schools should do, during this period outsiders were again telling the educators what to do.

While these discussions swirled around the press in the 1950s, school practitioners were faced with a much more immediate and practical dimension of the push for access: finding a place for each student in a decent school building for a full day and in a class that was not enormous with a teacher who was prepared to instruct. The principal problem was accommodating the "war babies" who began entering elementary schools just as the decade began and as the small cohort born in the depression was leaving. The year with the lowest birthrate in the United States was 1935. The children born that year would graduate from high school in about 1953, four years before the birthrate reached its new peak, leading to major enrollment increases. The consequence of these increases both in numbers of children and of their persistence in school was a dramatic rise in enrollments initially in the elementary schools and then year-by-year into the higher levels. Growth in the high schools was compounded by both the larger number of teenagers as well as their propensity to remain in school longer, completing high school in much greater numbers than their predecessors.

Total school enrollment grew from about 26 million at the end of World War II to 36 million by 1954 to a peak of more than 51 million in 1974 before declining

A Herblock cartoon satirizing parents' unreasonable demands of overcrowded, understaffed schools appeared in the *Washington Post*, 1955. *"Be Sure To Give Mine Special Attention" from* Herblock's Special for Today *(New York: Simon & Schuster, 1958); Image courtesy Prints & Photographs Division, Library of Congress*

to almost 45 million in 1983. In such circumstances parents sought space in school for their children, and educators frantically attempted to construct buildings, hire teachers, and find funds to provide for this need. Practical problems overwhelmed all others. For many local communities in the 1950s and 1960s the severe overcrowding of the schools and shortages of teachers, particularly for the rapidly expanding elementary schools, distracted them from other questions. The attentive school superintendent, however, also recognized growing public criticism of the academic proficiency of many students. Political leaders in southern states realized after May 17, 1954, that the U.S. Supreme Court had challenged their fundamental way of life, declaring racial segregation by law unconstitutional in *Brown* v. *Board of Education*, and the institution chosen to implement this decision was the public school. Eighth grader Dickie realized this, too, and he refused to accept it, as did many of his adult neighbors.

INCREASING KNOWLEDGE OF THE GIFTED

In the early years of this period most public critics, primarily academic professors and journalists, showed little interest in equal educational opportunity itself. Their focus was knowledge, not virtue. They demanded strengthening of the traditional academic curriculum, particularly for the college-bound students. They derided the life adjustment movement brought by the progressive educators, whose disdain for formal academic studies infuriated them. The critics' position strengthened dramatically when at the height of the Cold War the Soviet Union launched the first satellite, *Sputnik,* in October 1957. The United States had no *Sputnik* or its equivalent then. The Soviets' later achievement in April 1961, when they were able to hurl cosmonaut Yury Gagarin into orbit and bring him back safely, convinced many Americans that U.S. science and technology were deficient. The fault lay with the schools, the critics argued. The twice-defeated Democratic candidate for president, who was regarded as an "egghead" by many, Adlai Stevenson, however, believed this might be the stimulant that would inspire Americans to improve their children's education: "We needed *Sputnik*. It is sure proof that God has not despaired of us," he observed immediately after the launch.

Demand for more and better instruction in mathematics and science in the schools became a clarion call. This demand was initially supported by philanthropic foundations, particularly the Carnegie Corporation and the Ford Foundation, and the federal government, then a relative outsider to U.S. school programs, soon became involved. The National Science Foundation, created in 1950, burst upon the education scene with more than $14 million in 1957, rising to $134 million in 1968, funding mostly for new science education curricula and summer teacher institutes, a sum it did not reach again (in constant dollars) until 1993. The Eisenhower administration used the *Sputnik* opportunity to gain passage in Congress of the National Defense Education Act of 1958 (NDEA). The bill opened with the observation, "The Congress finds that an educational emergency exists and requires action by the federal government. Assistance will come from Washington to help develop as rapidly as possible those skills essential to the national defense." This legislation provided federal funds to support math, science, and foreign language instruction at the school and college levels. Inevitably these courses served the academically successful, disproportionately in affluent communities.

After World War II, service in the federal government, including the Department of Health, Education, and Welfare, still attracted many of what the journalist David Halberstam would subsequently term "the best and the brightest," a calling that has faded in recent years. Elliot Richardson fit that mold. Patrician to his toes, Richardson was born in Boston in 1920 and graduated from Harvard College in 1941 and its law school in 1947 and after two distinguished court clerkships, joined one of Boston's most prestigious law firms. Yet Richardson then chose government service, working first as assistant to the liberal Republican senator from Massachusetts, Leverett Saltonstall, before moving to his first tour of federal service at the Department of Health, Education, and Welfare, where as assistant secretary for legislation he was instrumental in gaining passage of NDEA. Richardson observed privately many years later that he had envisioned this legislation simply as a means of improving instruction in these fields and had used the Soviet threat to defense as a "hook" to get the legislation passed. Richardson subsequently served in Republican administrations as secretary of commerce, defense, and health, education and welfare. He resigned as attorney general when President Nixon told him to fire his friend, Harvard Law professor Archibald Cox, who was investigating Watergate.

Richardson and a fellow Bostonian, MIT vice president Vannevar Bush, whose book *Science: The Endless Frontier* stimulated the creation of the National Science Foundation, exemplified the new leadership among federal officials determining educational policy. They emphasized academic work of high quality, reflecting their own education at institutions that demanded such work. At the National Science Foundation and at the Department of Health, Education, and Welfare grants programs supported the finest scientific research in America, perhaps in the world. In education, Richardson pushed for programs that reemphasized rigorous intellectual classwork and research for selected students in subjects deemed essential to American security. Their interests were in potentially gifted scholars, not ordinary children.

When the Democrats came to power with the election of John F. Kennedy in 1960, a new group assumed leadership, and their attention turned less to increasing knowledge in the schools than to enhancing equality of educational opportunity. While both groups of federal officials of the fifties and sixties contained plenty of Yale and Harvard graduates, the Republicans paid more attention to knowledge while the Democrats concentrated on increasing the opportunities to acquire it. Without exception they were white men, though now some Catholics joined the Protestants. These federal officials, both Republicans and Democrats, however, shared few of the interests or experiences of Lucy Sprague Mitchell or Carleton Washburne.

FINDING THE GIFTED

Testing efforts, which had begun in school systems in the 1920s and were now widespread, gave school people the expectation that they could determine both their students' absolute intelligence as well as their achievement levels in different academic subjects. With these tools, they could identify the "gifted," who would be counted upon to keep the United States competitive with the Soviet Union.

These kinds of tests provided the basis for clustering students of apparent comparable achievement and/or ability in classes, called tracks, so that teachers could be under the assumption, if partly an illusion, that all their students were at the same level. Tracking worked best, of course, in large school systems where an individual school had multiple tiers with the top section for the "gifted" and the lower ones for students whose skill in a given subject was less evident, if evident at all. Removing the "gifted" from ordinary classes reduced expectations for the lower tracks, a sentiment that both teachers and students generally understood, accepted, and, thus, fulfilled. Similarly being selected as a teacher of the "gifted" meant an increase in prestige, a distinction sought by many good teachers who enjoyed working with able, motivated students. Consequently often the best teachers went to work with the "gifted," leaving less successful teachers with low expectations with the low achievers.

Programs for gifted students were more likely to be found in districts with affluent families or in large cities where white middle-class parents who still patronized the public school system wanted to be assured that their children would be so identified. New York City had had such classes and specialized schools (Hunter Model School, Townsend Harris High School, Bronx High School of Science, Stuyvesant High School) for the gifted for many years. By the 1950s such classes were nearly universal in New York City public schools. They were called SP classes (shorthand for "special progress"), and one could walk into a Manhattan junior high school in the 1950s and 1960s and by observing the predominant skin color of the class determine with some degree of precision whether this was a SP class or one of the lower tracked classes.

When the former president of Harvard turned educational prognosticator, James B. Conant, published his best-selling treatise, *The American High School Today*, in 1959, his principal argument was for the consolidation of small high schools into big ones with a minimum of one hundred students in the senior class. Consistent with the emphasis on special programs for the gifted and tracking for others, Conant wanted high schools to offer the College Entrance Examination Board's advanced placement classes and tests, enabling students who did well on them to demonstrate their learning and sometimes be exempted from introductory college courses. These classes would be available to "gifted" college-bound youth. Conant's plan enabled Harvard to identify able but remote applicants, such as the sturdy hockey player from Duluth who demonstrated achievement in math through success on advanced placement tests, a merger of commitment to the gifted with recognition of the need to identify them in unusual places. The plan was a less successful strategy for the 90-plus percent of the students who remained in the ordinary classes without access to the special ones. Nonetheless, the College Board, which administered the tests (for a fee), expanded dramatically from nearly 2,200 exams in 1956 to more than 178,000 in 1981 (two years before the national enthusiasm for achievement developed) to nearly 1,272,000 in 2000.

PUBLIC CRITICS CONDEMN SCHOOLS

But were the schools providing ordinary students with adequate academic preparation? "No," answered an unparalleled number of commentators. Bernard Iddings Bell, the author of the 1949 book *Crisis in Education: A Challenge to American Complacency* (which anticipated the rhetoric of *A Nation at Risk*), wrote in the introduction to Mortimer Smith's *And Madly Teach* (1949), "American education is so defective in theory and practice as seriously to threaten the long continuance of the way of life to further which this nation was founded." His focus was upon academic inadequacies precipitated by acceptance of the tenets of life adjustment education.

University of Illinois history professor Arthur Bestor developed this theme in two vitriolic attacks on public educators and their academic weaknesses, *Educational Wasteland: The Retreat from Learning in Our Public Schools* in 1953 (reissued in 1985, two years after publication of a similar critique, *A Nation at Risk*) and *The Restoration of Learning* in 1955. In the latter Bestor argued,

> To accomplish these high ends [the restoration of learning], the school must transmit to the public at large, not merely to its own students, a respect for knowledge and cultural achievement. If we are to have an intellectual life that is both democratic and worthy of democracy, the school must uphold for all men the ideal of disciplined intellectual effort.

Bestor believed the schools had failed in this important mission.

Bestor began his academic career on the faculty of Teachers College, Columbia University, where most of his colleagues were enthusiastic supporters of progressive education. He rarely referred to his earlier experience, but his two best-known works clearly reflect his dissatisfaction with the views of his colleagues of that period. As the titles of these two redundant works express, he believed that "learning," as defined by mastery of traditional subject matter, was no longer as important a priority in many American schools under the influence of "life adjustment education" as he believed that it should be.

Bestor attempted to correct the schools' deficiencies by founding the Council for Basic Education (CBE), of which he was president in 1956, the year after its ideological opposite, the Progressive Education Association, collapsed. In January 1958, the CBE criticized President Eisenhower's new aid to education proposal on the ground that "its administration would be in the hands of those professional educators who, by use of the 'soft' theory of education, are responsible for our present educational difficulties." Often a lonely voice in the fifties, sixties, and seventies calling for stronger academic programs in schools, the council closed its books in 2004, apparently unable to find a place for itself in the current debate about the subject it championed, academic achievement.

Others joined Bestor's crusade. Rudolf Flesch addressed parents in *Why Johnny Can't Read* (1955) about the failures of the schools to teach reading. Flesch recommended phonics (learning to read by sounding out the letters in a word) as opposed to the "look/see" method widely advocated at the time, which put a premium upon a student recognizing a new word in a context in which they could understand it. In 1958, as the federal education bill was being debated, *Life* magazine's cover story compared the school experiences of two sixteen-year-olds, Alexei Kutzkov of Moscow and Stephen Lapekas of Chicago, and found the Chicagoan's sadly inferior.

The iconoclastic admiral who brought us nuclear submarines, Hyman Rickover, turned his pen to education in this same period, publishing first a collection of speeches he had given in the mid-1950s as *Education and Freedom* in 1959, followed by *Swiss Schools and Ours: Why Theirs are Better* in 1962 and *American Education: A National Failure* in 1963. He, too, wanted schools and students that were stronger academically and believed that our national defense was dependent upon them, a common theme among the critics. Rickover, like Thomas Jefferson, saw American democracy resting on a strong public school system. He believed that the one that surrounded him was not strong because too few students excelled academically. In analytic prose mixed with personal commentary, Rickover decried ordinary schooling and its practitioners in frequent congressional testimony, thereby creating a national audience for his views.

A second stream of protest literature emerged in the following decade, led by two highly regarded journalists, Martin Mayer and Charles Silberman. They undertook their own analyses of what had now become an important public topic: schooling. Mayer's book *The Schools* was published in 1961 with this explanation on its cover, "The facts behind the controversies—why the American schools are as they are today." Mayer's literate, felicitous volume portrayed the American schools as burdened by bureaucracy but fundamentally strong. Published seven years after *Brown* v. *Board of Education*, the index includes no references to Negro, colored, segregation, or the *Brown* decision itself. Like most of the protest literature, the focus of attention was schooling for the white middle and upper class. Charles Silberman, on the other hand, in his earlier book, *Crisis in Black and White* (1964), recognized and alerted his reading public to racial issues in America, something no other widely read book on education had done to that time. Silberman's subsequent volume on education, *Crisis in the Classroom: The Remaking of American Education* (1970), written a tumultuous decade later, was more inclusive of the diversity of American educational experience and the varied challenges it presented. All three books were widely read and cited.

Coexisting within the genre of educational protest literature was a third stream, dominated by practitioners and psychologists who found existing schools stultifying and damaging to youth, much as the partisans of adjustment had. Beginning with A. S. Neill's *Summerhill* (1960), some of the ideas expressed in these volumes reminded one of the most halcyon days of child-centered schools of the 1920s, although Neill had founded his school, Summerhill, in England. During the exuberant sixties Edgar Z. Friedenberg pressed for greater attention to children's social and psychological development, believing it an essential prerequisite for intellectual activity. These authors, often termed "romantics," were unified in their critique of excessively bureaucratized and insensitive public schools but much less concerned with mastery of traditional academic subjects than Bestor's group. These practitioners and psychologists paid the greatest attention to affluent youth, just as the early adjustment group had, but Jonathan Kozol, with his remarkable *Death at an Early Age* (1967), shifted the focus to the children of the poor and the rigid, inhumane public schools in which they found themselves.

For the previous three decades, from 1920 to 1950, professors of education had led public discussion about education; now they came under heavy criticism for their efforts. Critics questioned their methods for preparing teachers, which James Conant described unflatteringly in *The Education of American Teachers* (1963) and James Koerner attacked viciously in *The Miseducation of American Teachers* (1963). These critics reflected considerable public dissatisfaction with the state of the American public schools and, particularly with the people responsible for them (principally school administrators, teachers, and professors of education). This dissatisfaction triggered efforts to create alternatives to regular schooling in the form of access to special educational programs within the public school system.

What was one to make of these different but vociferous critics? First, the public wanted its schools back and rejected the professional leadership provided by professors of education during the decades before World War II when matters other than schooling occupied the public. Second, those with strong academic interests themselves recognized that the curricula of many American schools in the wake of the adjustment era largely omitted the subject matter that had informed their youths, and presumably accounted for their present success. Third, the critics selected professors of education and their elementary and secondary school colleagues as the objects of their wrath because they had, in fact, had much more control over school policies in the interwar years than ordinarily, when they took orders from the broader society about the goals of schooling. Finally, educators did not have the political strength or access to the media and to power enjoyed by many of the critics.

The professors of education were still predominantly white men who were not regarded highly by their academic colleagues in other fields in their universities. The teachers were primarily women, and many people did not take their views seriously even though parents might lobby intensely to get "the wonderful Mrs. X" for their third-grade child's classroom teacher. Ultimately what was missing was an understanding of why and how Mrs. X was so wonderful. Without that knowledge critics flailed about, filled with concern about current practices but unable to articulate how to achieve the transformation of universal academic achievement for all children combined with the qualities of integrity, ingenuity, creativity, teamwork, and fair play necessary for participation in the American democracy and economy. Articulating those challenges was left to the next era.

PROFESSIONAL EDUCATORS SEEK LEGITIMACY

Some professors of education fought back, but their target was not clear. Should they attack the teachers and administrators who were their graduates? Should they attack their senior colleagues who had taught these school people? Should they attack the public critics who faulted them and their presumed ideology? What was the case they could make? With whom could they ally themselves?

The Young Turks, as the *New York Times* columnist Fred Hechinger dubbed them, emerged on the Teachers College faculty in the late 1950s, led by historian Lawrence Cremin, an intense and charismatic teacher, prolific author, and consummate architect of increasing the status of education in America.

Cremin and his fellow reformers led the efforts to bring stronger academic standards to the study of education itself by aligning themselves with their disciplinary colleagues in the arts and sciences. Cremin identified himself as a historian, winning both Bancroft and Pulitzer Prizes in history, and hired colleagues who defined themselves as historians, philosophers, sociologists, political scientists, economists, or psychologists and who applied that discipline to the study of education. They saw themselves as researchers in education, not practitioners of it, and attempted to dissociate themselves from their fellow professors of education who sought involvement with schoolteachers and administrators. Deploring these colleagues' uncritical acceptance of a simplified and bowdlerized Deweyan message of "growth" as the end of education, some brought an intellectual isolation and, occasionally, arrogance to their work that ignored the complexities and significance of instruction in either knowledge or virtue. This group largely redefined educational research, improving it substantially.

By the early 1960s many of the leading professors of education sought an alliance with academics who were playing an increasingly important role in their field. These education professors sought to assuage the critics' complaints about the inadequacies of the schools by joining forces with some of the most prestigious university professors whose research included educational issues but who were based not in schools of education but in academic departments. Following the model of the prestigious National Academy of Sciences, an honorary group for leading scientists offering advice to the federal government on scientific matters, Cremin, with the help of former Harvard president James Conant and Israel Scheffler, a professor of philosophy and education at Harvard, organized the National Academy of Education in 1965.

Of the original group in the National Academy of Education only three identified themselves with education alone. All the other members were best known for their disciplinary work in history, sociology, economics, or psychology, presumably the source of their professional identity, not education. The academy helped to raise the standards for educational research, certainly a desirable and beneficial goal. However, by attempting to find legitimacy within the academic disciplines, the academy often missed the fundamental issues affecting education: poverty, racism, and anti-intellectualism. They were strongest on the last.

While the professors argued about research disciplines, policy, and methodologies, they failed to recognize the profound shift occurring in education as a result of the *Brown* decision. The trustees of the universities and colleges, however, were apparently more attuned to the issue, particularly at Teachers College, which appointed John Fischer the new dean in 1959 and made him president in 1962. Fischer was not a researcher but rather an experienced and respected administrator who had served as a superintendent of the Baltimore public schools, one of the first segregated city school systems to enroll black and white children in the same classrooms after the *Brown* decision. Fischer retired in 1974 after a period of honorable service but without focusing the institution on the racial issues engulfing education in his New York City neighborhood and the nation as a whole. Neither did his successor, historian Lawrence Cremin, the former Young Turk. Fundamental institutional change comes hard.

Neither Fischer nor Cremin was able to resolve the basic dilemma for schools of education: striking the appropriate balance between increasing knowledge about education and improving its practice. Both are essential and reciprocal; each needs the other in order to flourish. Yet within the same faculty the culture of research was often at odds with the culture of practice, and administrative leadership could not overcome this chasm. The losers were the children and the communities in which they would live and work.

The situation at other leading schools of education, such as Chicago, Harvard, and Stanford, was similar during this period. Faculties and their administrations appeared most concerned about achieving legitimacy in the eyes of their academic colleagues in the traditional disciplines. Their concern was well placed as senior administrators at Yale, Duke, and Johns Hopkins eliminated their schools of education, while Berkeley and Harvard considered it, and administrators at Chicago downgraded their school of education to the status of department within a broader faculty of social science. As a consequence, focus on teacher education declined at these institutions, and schools, such as Harvard, Chicago, and Johns Hopkins, that had had leading masters of arts in teaching (MAT) programs in the 1950s and 1960s had dropped them by the mid-1970s. Research about education, subject to rigorous disciplinary and methodological standards, became de rigueur. Concern about the practice of education or the preparation of practitioners faded.

Teacher education programs became located nearly exclusively in institutions with either open admissions or only moderately selective admissions standards, thus assuring that many future teachers did not enter their profession with strong academic backgrounds. For elementary teachers this was particularly true as most majored in education, thus depriving them of an academic major and often of a strong base in the liberal arts. High school teachers were more likely to have an academic major but often in a single discipline when they were expected to teach several subjects. For example, a teacher who had majored in biology might be expected to instruct students not only in biology but also in various levels of general science, chemistry, and possibly physics or mathematics. In hiring, preference was given to individuals who were certified, those who had completed the "professional education sequence" allowing them to be licensed; less attention was given to whether the aspiring teacher had ever studied or mastered the subjects to be taught. This was anti-intellectualism at its worst and, of course, played into the hands of critics concerned with schools' lack of emphasis on knowledge.

FUNDING FOR ENHANCING CURRICULUM

In spite of the shortages and inadequate preparation of teachers, national emphasis shifted away from them and to the curriculum. The government and private foundation leaders who drove this shift sought not school of education faculty but rather professors of academic disciplines to create new curricula. Organized by the National Science Foundation and spending more than $1.5 billion between 1954 and 1975, physicists, chemists, biologists, and mathematicians developed curricula and trained teachers in summer institutes. Physicist Jerrold Zacharias at MIT initiated these efforts with the Physical Sciences Study Committee

(PSSC), attracting leading American physicists, then the kings of the sciences following their World War II contributions, to advise on physics curriculum for high school students. The historian of science and education John Rudolph insightfully describes their approach to and development of texts, filmstrips, a teacher's manual, laboratory work, and examinations and their confidence in their ability to make this all work, as well as their radar experiments in World War II, in his compelling *Scientists in the Classroom* (2002).

Stimulated by the same public concerns that had led to the passage of NDEA in 1958, these efforts were largely intended for the select college preparatory students who took these science courses in high school, a minority of their age group. The "new math," which was intended to replace arithmetic for the many, was also the most widely criticized. When the NSF ventured into anthropology with MACOS (Man, A Course of

In 1960, students engage in the "new math," developed at the University of Illinois. Following the launch of *Sputnik* in 1957, university professors, particularly in the sciences and math, developed demanding new curricula for "gifted and talented" students. *Photograph courtesy of the University of Illinois at Urbana-Champaign Archives, Record Series Number 39/2/20, Box 99*

Study) it soon evoked popular wrath as children were taught that Eskimos sent their elderly out to die on ice floes. Many Americans (presumably older ones, particularly) did not want their children taught that!

Jerome Bruner, a penetrating and prolific psychologist then at Harvard, captured the issue succinctly in his 1960 volume, *The Process of Education*. Bruner's book summarized a Ford Foundation–funded summer seminar in 1959 at Woods Hole, Massachusetts, which had involved thirty-one leading scholars in academic disciplines discussing school curriculum. Only three of the participants had significant experience in schools. Bruner acknowledged immediately, "The first and most obvious problem is how to construct curricula that can be taught by ordinary teachers to ordinary students and that at the same time reflect clearly the basic or underlying principles of various fields of inquiry." He went on to state that, "the best minds in any particular discipline must be put to work on this task." As Bruner continued, "Only by the use of our best minds in devising curricula will we bring the fruits of scholarship and wisdom to the student just beginning his studies." The "best minds," identified as professors of the academic disciplines, not education, at prestigious universities, hypothesized that "any subject can be taught effectively in some intellectually honest form to any child at any stage of development." This view legitimated the "spiral" notion of curriculum. In this practice, teachers taught the same basic idea year after year, ostensibly at more advanced levels each year but in reality often just repeating the previous year's lesson. Slow students, thus, had an opportunity to learn the material on the second or third try while the quick students became bored.

Inevitably such "best minds" were more interested in and knowledgeable about their disciplines (after all, that was how they were chosen for the seminar) than they were about the working conditions in which "ordinary teachers" labored or about the academic competence and understanding of such teachers themselves or about the interests and motivations of "ordinary students" for studying this material. As Jerrold Zacharias, the MIT physicist who developed a high school physics curriculum, explained, "We had to establish a first-class collection of stuff for the intellectual elite of the country, no question." Zacharias sought to accomplish this with a group who would Americanize intellectual life showing that "a physicist was *not* a Hungarian with a briefcase talking broken English but . . . somebody who spoke English with no accent, who was one of the boys."

Yet for the child who was expected to learn this material, the culture of the school and the academic and pedagogical skills of the teacher were undoubtedly more important than ascertaining the underlying structure of subject matter embedded in the curriculum. The "best minds" were both less interested in and less competent to address those issues. Yet the education professors who sought status from their university colleagues who comprised the "best minds" were reluctant to challenge their views.

Although Bruner and his NSF-funded colleagues recognized at least rhetorically the need to prepare teachers to use the new curricula, the contemporary alternative effort was to create a "teacher proof" curriculum, largely designed by companies or divisions of large corporations, such as General Learning at Time/Life publishing or Science Research Associates at IBM. Early work in computer-assisted instruction led by Harvard psychologist B. F. Skinner and later by Stanford psychologists Patrick Suppes and Richard Atkinson followed much the same principle. The rationale behind these efforts was that the materials themselves could organize children's learning without significant intervention by the teacher. The underlying but unstated assumption, of course, was that the teachers were not competent to instruct the students effectively.

The days when little Victor Albjerg thought he could "be somebody" by becoming a rural schoolteacher were long gone. Teaching declined in prestige profoundly in post–World War II America, partly as a result of losing the "hidden subsidy" of able white women, blacks, and Jews whose previously limited vocational opportunities had pushed many to teaching. When the professions, including college teaching, began to open to them, many left the schools. As complicated certification requirements evolved through the twenties and thirties, able men who might have taught for a few years directly after graduating from high school or college before returning to complete their education were barred from the profession. This largely silent but widely understood criticism of the teaching forces was undoubtedly a factor in the decisions of the leading schools of education to eliminate their teacher education programs. These institutions wanted to concentrate their resources on activities held in higher esteem by persons they considered important, namely their presidents, provosts, and colleagues in the academic disciplines.

RESEARCH ABOUT EDUCATION BUT NOT SCHOOLING

With scientists, not educators, undertaking the major curriculum reforms and with the recognition that the status of school teaching was declining, the major schools of education all turned to an emphasis on research, an activity they thought would enhance their professional status and be congenial to and respected by their liberal arts colleagues. Yet this, too, was widely criticized when the research did not meet the "standards of the disciplines."

At the best universities most of the research about education focused on many "educational" subjects but not on issues of schooling. At the time schooling was in bad repute with leading educational researchers. Lawrence Cremin, for example, wrote about the "many agencies that educate," correctly emphasizing the substantial educational influences on young people other than schooling, including families, communities, religious organizations, museums, and media. Johns Hopkins sociologist James Coleman, drawn to research on education by a grant from the U.S. Office of Education, concluded that families and communities were more important educational influences than schools. Progressive educators looking at the Eight Year Study had reported this finding without realizing it, taking the success of the affluent students in their study as a justification for their new pedagogy. As if that were not enough to diminish the role of schooling, sociologist Christopher Jencks and his colleagues published *Inequality* in 1972, a study revealing that schooling alone did not overcome the influence of social class in predicting students' social mobility. The cynic, of course, might have inquired, "Who ever thought that it would?" The issue, however, was "how much can good schooling help the poor?" That had rarely been contemplated. Jencks's initial working title for the study had been "The Limits of Schooling."

Essentially the debate about the role of schools of education in highly selective universities was an argument among white men who themselves had prospered in school and in their profession and believed that their success was entirely based on their demonstrated merit. Few had experienced the culture of low expectations that enmeshed many white women and minorities, who were still unusual among tenured ranks of major universities. When women were on the faculty, they were primarily in the least prestigious departments, such as teacher education or curriculum and instruction.

Thus, the white men in the low status education departments sought equivalence with the white men in the academic disciplines who left their highly regarded work in the sciences or mathematics or history to consider how their favorite subjects might be organized for young students. Unlike the men a generation or two before who addressed the problem of education, most of these men had no experience teaching school. Their school experience was limited to their own schooling or their children's schooling. Given their professional position, school was likely to have been a successful experience for them and their children were likely enrolled in a favored school district. Few of these men were much interested in "ordinary schools": how they were organized, how teachers and administrators should be prepared and assisted, or what conditions needed to exist in a school for children to learn and develop. Their silence was overwhelming on the fundamental issue of how to desegregate. The focus remained on access to special programs, particularly curricular innovations mostly though not exclusively intended for the college-bound or "gifted" student. Initially, their response was to the public critics, such as Arthur Bestor, who resembled them, not to the civil rights activists, such as Thurgood Marshall, with whom they did not identify. Recognizing the inadequacies of the life adjustment schools, they stood foursquare for improving instruction but did not study how to make the necessary changes. They left civic virtue to others.

DESEGREGATION

Historically Washington, D.C., had been a locale that had meant relatively little to educators. During the first half of the twentieth century—except for a single piece of federal legislation on vocational education, the Smith-

Hughes Act of 1917, and occasional pronouncements capturing broad public sentiments, such as the Seven Cardinal Principles in 1918 or the Commission on Life Adjustment Education in 1947—school people and professors of education regarded schools as a local and state enterprise. "Local control" underlay all discussions about education along with the bromide that "education was beyond politics." This situation changed dramatically in 1954, two years into Republican president Dwight Eisenhower's first term, when the Supreme Court unanimously decided *Brown* v. *Board of Education,* a case that certainly did not reflect either the president's view or universal public sentiment in the United States. *Brown* held that legal segregation of schools by race, a practice common in all the southern states by law and in many northern states by tradition and housing patterns, was unconstitutional. Led by Chief Justice Earl Warren, the Court took a Topeka, Kansas, case, added cases from three other states plus the District of Columbia, and finally spoke unanimously on May 17, 1954,

> We conclude that in the field of public education the doctrine of "separate but equal" has no place. Separate educational facilities are inherently unequal. Therefore, we hold that the plaintiffs . . . are by reason of the segregation complained of, deprived of the equal protection of the laws guaranteed by the Fourteenth Amendment.

A year later the Court, again unanimous, ordered that schools should be desegregated "with all deliberate speed." Deliberation, rather than speed, characterized the states' and most communities' reaction to the decision.

The clarity of purpose expressed in the 1954 decision heartened many Americans, particularly blacks and sympathetic whites. But the ambiguity of the 1955 decision, which determined implementation of *Brown,* that is, what would really happen, engulfed the nation in controversy. Initially a southern problem, desegregation became a northern one as well when federal courts pressured districts to move children from one school to another to achieve "racial balance" a decade or so later. Today polling data reveal broad U.S. support for the principle of desegregation, but much greater uncertainty exists about the practice of it. The course has not been easy for the educators, mostly schoolteachers and administrators, who have attempted, often under court order, to bring together children whose parents do not wish to be brought together. We have expected our children to do what adults could not.

For most of the decade following the 1954 and 1955 decisions, district courts and southern school systems skirmished around the issue. Political leaders in the South, particularly governors in Arkansas (Orval Faubus), Mississippi (Ross Barnett), Alabama (George Wallace), and Virginia (Lindsay Almond), undertook various obstructive tactics to avoid compliance with the Court's decision.

President Eisenhower's enthusiasm for the decisions was extremely limited. In 1957, however, Eisenhower reluctantly ordered federal troops to Little Rock to quell rioting there. President Kennedy took similar action, also reluctantly, with federal marshals in Mississippi in 1962. National political parties, including the old Democratic coalition of liberals, urban working class, and southerners, split apart as South Carolina's Strom Thurmond joined the Republican Party in 1964, and George Wallace ran for president as an independent segregationist, gaining considerable support in the primaries in 1968.

For those of us then teaching in segregated schools, as I was in Norfolk, Virginia, this issue overtook all others in our professional lives. In my case, my school, Maury High School, and all other white Norfolk public schools closed in September 1958, rather than admit any black students. Most children were at loose ends, a worry to parents and the community, since Norfolk at that time had few nonpublic schools. The public schools remained closed for a full term before reopening in 1959, under pressure from the federal district court. Teaching civics in such circumstances was trying indeed, though the new name given to that course—problems of democracy—seemed oddly appropriate.

These dramas at the schoolhouse door played themselves out in the context of several factors. First, the 1960s civil rights movement, with its initial alliances between liberal whites and blacks who favored desegregation, was followed by the separatism exemplified

Maury High School, Norfolk, Virginia, reopened in 1959 with a lonely black student isolated from his white classmates in the school auditorium. *Staff photo. Courtesy of* Norfolk Virginian Pilot

by the Black Panthers, for whom integration was not a goal. Second, the Supreme Court retreated from its willingness to enforce desegregation, particularly across city lines, after the Nixon appointees joined the Court in the early 1970s. Third, the civil rights movement's efforts to desegregate schools by race occurred simultaneously with the emergence of the women's movement, which expanded job opportunities outside education for the predominantly female teaching force. Some women became school administrators, a rare occurrence in earlier years. White males, traditionally the leaders in public education, found their traditional power and authority challenged by individuals, women and minorities, whose experience growing up in America had been quite different from theirs. That was not easy either.

In 1970 for the first time blacks assumed school superintendencies in major cities, with Marcus Foster in Oakland and Hugh Scott in Washington, D.C., both deeply troubled school systems. The same year California elected a black superintendent of public instruction, Wilson Riles. Alonzo Crim went to Atlanta in 1973, the first major southern city to have a black superintendent. During the late 1970s and 1980s nearly all the large urban districts (New York, Chicago, Los Angeles, Boston, San Francisco, Baltimore, Houston, Miami, and Milwaukee)—all of which faced a multitude of educational, political, and fiscal difficulties—hired superintendents of color. Many were women, a much higher percentage than among white superintendents: Barbara Sizemore who was later replaced by Floretta McKenzie in Washington, D.C., and Ruth Love in Oakland and subsequently Chicago. Superintendents of color did not find themselves in demand in affluent districts with high scoring students; rather, they were sought in districts where hope had been extinguished for many of the students.

School people were left to struggle with the monumental issue of desegregation largely on their own, initially. Astonishingly, at the places where schools might have expected some help, namely the schools of education that prepared their staffs, relatively little assistance emerged for a decade or two. Many of the leading ones were still caught up in the emphasis on research and the attempt to prove to their liberal arts colleagues that they too could be considered among "the best minds." When the New York City schoolteachers went out on strike for three successive years in the late 1960s over issues of community control of schools and teacher authority, pitting black community members against a union leadership that was largely white and Jewish, little help in resolving the crisis came from Teachers College. Similarly when the Boston schools were forced under court order to desegregate in 1974, Harvard initially was not notably helpful in assisting that difficult process. By the end of the decade both institutions had made considerable efforts, largely through new faculty and administrative appointments, to turn their attention to the problem that the public recognized as the premier educational issue of the time: desegregation. The focus shifted rapidly from efforts to participate in designing elegant and academically rigorous curricula for gifted students. Rather, the perceived national problem was no longer a shortage of expert talent but rather the need for more help with "basic skills," a problem for both black and white students and one that had not been taken seriously before.

Black educators, particularly in the South where the desegregation mandate became most pressing, however, paid close attention to these matters immediately, as historians Vanessa Siddle Walker and Michael Fultz have explained. Their future depended on how desegregation worked in practice. For many, the democratic ideal that desegregation represented, and which they endorsed, remained far distant from the reality they confronted: lost jobs, lost schools, and lost presence in their communities.

ELEMENTARY AND SECONDARY EDUCATION ACT OF 1965

Initially leadership for desegregation was lacking in both the Congress and the Executive Branch in Washington. When John F. Kennedy was elected in 1960, he understood that federal support for NDEA, passed in 1958, was a much safer stance to take on education than one dealing with desegregation, which he and his brother Robert, the attorney general, recognized was politically explosive both for the country and for the Democratic Party. Consistent with that view, he selected a philosopher from Utah, Sterling McMurrin, as the commissioner of the U.S. Office of Education, then the highest education official in the federal government although traditionally a very weak post politically. This was not perceived to be a stellar job, reporting as it did through several bureaucratic layers to the secretary of health, education, and welfare.

Professor McMurrin returned to Utah the following year, allegedly frustrated by his experience. Kennedy then appointed as commissioner a Harvard classmate, Francis Keppel, dean of the Harvard Graduate School of Education and a protégé of former Harvard president James B. Conant. Keppel brought new vitality to the U.S. Office of Education, and he and his successor, Harold Howe II, created the forces that brought desegregation to many schools.

The implements Keppel and Howe used to effect this transformation were ideas, money, and political skills. Essentially what they did was to link Lyndon Johnson's Great Society legislation to both school desegregation

Francis Keppel (right), former dean of the Harvard Graduate School of Education, with James B. Conant, president of Harvard from 1933 to 1953 and frequent critic of American schools, at Keppel's retirement dinner on January 11, 1963. Keppel went on to become commissioner of the U.S. Office of Education, where he would secure passage of the Elementary and Secondary Education Act of 1965. *Harvard University Archives. Call # UAV 605.270.5 p*

and federal aid to education. The Civil Rights Act of 1964, through Title VI, permitted the federal government to cut off federal funds intended for school districts that violated the Civil Rights Act by maintaining segregated schools. Until 1965 most school districts would not have found that an enormous loss as most school money came either from local or state governments. However, when the Elementary and Secondary Education Act of 1965 (ESEA) was finally passed by Congress and signed by President Johnson, each congressional district in the country was assured some federal money through Title I, which paid for "compensatory education" programs for children in low-income areas. The percent of school funding that came from the federal government jumped from 4.4 percent in 1964 to 8.8 percent in 1968 to a peak of 9.8 percent at the end of the Carter administration in 1980. The money was proportionately distributed to districts that needed it most, those who had concentrations of students from families below the official poverty line. These were children who were likely to be doing poorly in school and whose families were unlikely to be paying much in local taxes. Enactment of ESEA provided the federal government with some leverage. Local districts wanted the federal money, and to get it they had to avoid being in violation of the Civil Rights Act.

Two enormous political hurdles had to be overcome to reach this point: a general federal aid to education bill that was large enough to interest both local school personnel and members of Congress had to be passed, and its resources had to be linked in some way with efforts to desegregate the schools. The task confronting Francis Keppel when he took up his duties as commissioner of the U.S. Office of Education was to build the coalition that could gain passage of ESEA. Federal aid to elementary and secondary schools had been a matter of discussion, but no action, since World War II. As Keppel used to say, four Rs stood in its way: Race, Republicans, Roman Catholics, and Reds. Keppel had to deal with each to secure its passage.

Each of the four was a political hot potato, and everyone in the White House from the president to his staff was eager for Keppel, not them, to handle it. Race interfered with enactment of the federal legislation because southern Democrats rightly worried that such aid would be used to force integration. Religion was a problem as powerful Catholic interests in northern cities refused to support a bill that would not provide aid for parochial schools, something many Protestants, Jews, and secular liberals opposed as a violation of the principle of the separation of church and state. Finally, many Republicans and conservative Democrats, painting federal aid to education as a socialist or "Red" assault on local school control, pointed to the Tenth Amendment to the Constitution as reserving education as an issue for the states. Keppel faced a formidable concentration of powerful political opponents in seeking support for the passage of ESEA.

Fortunately for Keppel and the Johnson administration, 1965 was a propitious time to break this historic logjam. Both the 1964 Civil Rights Act and the *Brown* v. *Board of Education* decision had dealt with the racial issue. Keppel, along with a young domestic policy advisor in the White House, Joseph A. Califano Jr., sidestepped the religion issue by agreeing with the Catholic bishops to accept a compromise based on the "child benefit" theory, which allowed children in the parochial schools to receive certain benefits but prohibited the schools from getting direct funds. The Democratic landslide accompanying Johnson's 1964 reelection provided handsome working majorities of Democrats in both the House and Senate, giving the White House enormous legislative clout. The Johnson administration used this advantage to great effect, reflecting the lessons of the "master of the Senate," now the president of the United States.

Johnson sent the draft ESEA legislation up to Capitol Hill and demanded that it be enacted immediately, unchanged. Within ninety days he was signing the legislation, which, except for an evaluation requirement urged by Senator Wayne Morse, a former Wisconsin and Oregon law school professor, and added at the last minute by then senator Robert F. Kennedy of New York, was identical to the bill submitted by the White House. Then, the questions became: how to get the money to the school districts, something the federal government had never done before, and how to assure that the districts spent it on the intended children, something the federal officials feared they would not do. Questions about whether the money spent would increase these children's learning came later.

Who was this man Keppel who managed what had eluded others for so long? The son of the former dean of Columbia College and president of the Carnegie Corporation, a graduate of Groton and Harvard College with his only graduate work being a year in Rome studying sculpture, Keppel seemed an unlikely choice to lead the parade on behalf of better schools for low-income children, which was the centerpiece of ESEA. A Harvard classmate of Elliot Richardson, Keppel was a Democrat, not a Republican, though, as a member of Boston's elite Somerset Club, he had some of the same patrician qualities as Richardson, who was his friend.

While president of the Carnegie Corporation, Keppel's father, Frederick, had commissioned the Swedish social scientist Gunnar Myrdal to assemble a team of young scholars, many of whom were black, to develop the most comprehensive analysis of the race issue in the United States. In 1944, the team published *An American Dilemma: The Negro Problem and Modern Democracy.* Myrdal argued eloquently that the "American Creed" held the values of democracy and fairness to all, but that racial segregation as practiced in the United States violated the creed's most fundamental tenets. One of the senior Keppel's regrets was that this towering work failed to receive the attention it merited because it was published at the height of World War II when Americans' interests were elsewhere. His son, who became a trustee of Carnegie Corporation after his father's retirement, had grasped the importance both of the race issue and its implications for American democracy.

Due to a lack of sufficient funding, the ESEA funds while authorized for all grades were concentrated on the early elementary grades and were used to provide yet more special programs, this time termed "compensatory education." These were aimed at children enrolled in schools with a high incidence of poverty among their students. Nearly every member of Congress had at least a school or two like that in his district.

Additional instruction, however it was conducted (either within the classroom or more commonly in "pull-out" sections), would benefit the child, the argument went. Many argued about the desirability of federal funds going to local districts with the caveat that the schools provide special programs, thus raising the specter of "federal control." In order to avoid that issue, the U.S. Office of Education (USOE) did not try to determine the content of the programs, emphasizing rather that the funding stream would provide the means to make "equal educational opportunity" a reality instead of a slogan. Politically that compromise was necessary; furthermore, no one at USOE or anywhere else knew how to ensure literacy for all.

Obviously the other major obstacle to creating "equal educational opportunity" was the segregation of the schools. While "separate but equal" may have been struck down as a matter of law, segregated schools continued to exist, as a matter of fact, with the tacit and often open support of local elected officials, now primarily as a result of resegregation and housing policy. Initially prodded by considerable court pressure through the 1968 decision in Virginia *Green* v. *County School Board of New Kent County* and the 1971 case in North Carolina *Swann* v. *Charlotte-Mecklenburg Board of Education*, southern communities moved to reduce the racial isolation of some of their schools. Gradually the pressure moved to northern cities, many of which now had a majority school enrollment of children of color. Before Keppel could make much progress on this increasingly important issue, national politics intervened again. Keppel left the commissionership in 1965 after a tiff over the segregation of Chicago's public schools in which President Lyndon Johnson and his staff worried more about offending a prominent Democrat, Chicago mayor Richard Daley, than they did about achieving school desegregation in his city, a task that has largely eluded Johnson's successors.

Keppel's successor, Harold Howe II, came to his task with verve, charm, intelligence, and a prodigious capacity for work. He needed all those qualities. Grandson of the founder of Hampton Institute (one of the early colleges established for blacks in Virginia) and son of a Presbyterian minister, who was also head of Hampton Institute in the 1930s when Howe was a teenager, "Doc" Howe did not come from the ranks of the teachers college establishment. Also a graduate of an elite prep school and Yale College, with a master's degree in history from Columbia, Howe was less patrician in his bearing and considerably less sartorial in his appearance than either Richardson or Keppel, favoring L.L. Bean as his couturier. Unlike Keppel, Howe brought substantial experience as a schoolteacher and administrator in Massachusetts, Ohio, New York, and North Carolina to his new federal responsibilities. Like Keppel, he was playful with ideas, and passionately committed to improving the education of low-income children, including blacks. He wrote extensively, always disassociating himself from the world of educational researchers, and he spoke and wrote with clarity and style that eluded most of the professional educators.

Howe needed all the charm he could muster to get the southern states to begin desegregation. Aided by the Courts' decisions and by the leverage of Title VI of the Civil Rights Act, Howe managed during his commissionership to preside over substantial desegregation of southern schools. (School districts did not get the federal ESEA or other money if courts found them inadequate in their desegregation efforts.) When he left, fired by incoming president Richard Nixon in 1969, he

Harold Howe II (right), commissioner of education from 1965 to 1969, speaking to President Lyndon Baines Johnson (left), at a time of intense debate regarding the use of federal funds to compel desegregation, primarily in southern communities, after passage of the 1964 Civil Rights Act. *National Education Association, Joe DiDio. Courtesy of Special Collections, Monroe C. Gutman Library, Harvard Graduate School of Education*

could look with pride over changes in the organization and governance of many southern schools. In the historically legally segregated South, the percentage of black children attending schools with whites jumped from 11 percent in 1964–1965 to 84 percent in 1970–1971.

NEW WORLD OF EDUCATIONAL POLICY

For Keppel and for Howe initially it was enough to get the rules changed. Subsequently they became very concerned about the quality of educational experiences, particularly for low-income children. From their positions in adjacent offices at the Harvard Graduate School of Education in the 1980s, often engulfed in the smoke from the dark cigars they favored, both pushed hard to translate the access for which they had fought so hard to become the achievement that had eluded these children for so long.

Keppel and Howe, like many of their New Deal predecessors, devised policy solutions by relying on their knowledge and their principles, not a bad combination when one was as wise and just as they. But by the 1960s when substantial federal programs in many fields were being proposed or initiated, both common sense as well as responsible government required that some analysis be done of the likely effects of these programs. The Great Society and War on Poverty of the Johnson administration from 1963 to 1968 was awash in such new programs. Exiles from the Johnson administration, such as McGeorge Bundy and Howe, left to join private foundations, especially the Ford Foundation, to augment with private funds the work they had done previously with public money. The Ford Foundation's signature issue in education was school finance reform. Their particular concern was the disparity between districts with concentrations of children from low-income families where per pupil expenditures were low and those districts, typically suburbs, with high-income families and high per pupil expenditures. They believed that changes in policy would also change practice accordingly and quickly. Changing practice turned out to be a lot more complicated.

One vital consequence of the funding decisions was the emergence of two new university specialties, public policy and evaluation. Together they closely linked the government, which authorized, funded, and administered the programs, with the academics or independent researchers who developed the specialty of programmatic evaluation. Before this we had judgment; now we had the science of evaluation.

"Policy studies" emerged as the new prescriptive field, combining what philosophers thought ought to be done with what historians believed had been done and what contemporary leaders wanted to do now. Policy was about programs to be established, incentives to be embedded, politics to be recognized, and money to be spent.

Education fit beautifully into these emerging disciplines and methodologies. The period of access entailed development of new policies and programs to supplement the various failings of the ailing general education system. The idea was that if you got the policy right, then everything else would fall into place. Problems of implementation came later; those were practitioner issues.

Leading public servants became "policymakers." Making the policy was the high status task, not implementing it. Typically formulating the policy included some recognition of research on the subject, though the research findings rarely determined the policy. The research was, of course, limited by the strictures of the research design. Inevitably the policy was neither comprehensive nor definitive in deciding precisely what needed to be done to solve the problem it intended to address. Policy was supplemented by "regulations," which flowed from congressional legislation that the executive branch staff, sometimes in concert with congressional staff, typically devised. Many of these staffers' school experiences were limited to their own or their children's schooldays, which gave them an illusion of understanding these institutions.

School administrators came to fear the "regs," which became the bane of the recipient's existence because they typically constricted the ways in which the funds could be spent and prescribed the accounting necessary for justifying the expenditures. The reason, of course, was to provide accountability for these public funds. Thus, the consequence for the school administrator was that the funds coming to support instruction—initially from the federal government for low-income students but later from both federal and state governments for various special programs—were so hobbled by restrictions and dramatically increasing federal, state, and local bureaucratic hierarchies that they often could not be spent in the most efficacious manner, or so many alleged.

Perhaps the best known example of this problem was the decision by many school districts to use the Title I funds from ESEA for supplementary instruction only for "pullout programs" in which the eligible children were taken from their regular classroom and given additional instruction elsewhere. Little thought was given either to what these students missed in the regular class or what stigmatism they might feel being taken away from their classmates. Nor did administrators consider whether such obviously remedial instruction would be as valuable for them as enriched instruction with more advanced classmates supplemented by a little tutoring on the side. The reason, of course, that the programs developed this way was that it was much easier to trace the funds used for pullout programs than in classrooms with integrated and improved instruction.

An additional challenge to school administrators during this period was the increasing unionization of teachers and other school personnel. The National Education Association, representing more than 90 percent of public school teachers, gradually transformed itself from a professional association to a collective bargaining agent for teachers. The American Federation of Teachers, representing the balance of the teachers, always allied itself clearly with the American labor movement and, therefore, supported both bargaining and strikes. While bringing important benefits of salary increases and job security to teachers, unionization also increased the bureaucratic nature of many school transactions, thus reducing teachers' and administrators' flexibility to arrange more challenging educational experiences for the children, an immense loss.

EVALUATIONS EMERGE

The new industry that developed as a consequence of all these policy and programmatic initiatives, evaluation, failed to explain fully both *whether* the program worked and *why* it did or did not work. Generally the evaluators were much better on the "whether" question than on the "why." The question of whether the program worked fit existing research designs and was more amenable to a quantitative analysis, such as the program reached 57.8 percent of the eligible recipients. Policymakers also wanted to know if their goal had been achieved: had the policy reached the appropriate individuals in sufficient quantity and quality to have the desired effect? But the latter question, why the policy worked or failed to do so, was much more important in facilitating replication of a valuable program or correcting one that was failing. Existing research designs did not lend themselves to answering that question easily.

One of the leading educational researchers of the era, sociologist James S. Coleman, became one of the early academic evaluators, as a consequence of the requirement that the Civil Rights Act of 1964 be "evaluated." Two years later, on the Saturday of the fourth of July weekend, when Keppel and Howe prayed that few would be reading the morning papers, Coleman reported in *Equality of Educational Opportunity* that student academic achievement was less related to the characteristics of the school (financing, teacher's salaries, building facilities—all items that could be improved with money, which the federal government had) than it was to the social composition of the student body.

Mixing middle-class children with low-income ones appeared to be a stimulus to academic improvement, particularly for the low-income children. This was bad news for the bureaucrats since their toolkit did not contain the instruments needed to accomplish this task. They could add money, but they could not easily move the middle-class children into schools with the poor ones, although the desegregation decisions before Nixon got his appointees on the Court tried to do just that.

What Howe could not assert—and what he had never promised—was that student academic achievement would rise in the desegregated schools, though many black families had initially welcomed desegregated schools because they believed that in such institutions their children would have an opportunity to get a better education. Results from the National Assessment of Educational Progress (NAEP), the national testing program Senator Robert F. Kennedy had required for his support of ESEA, revealed significant disparities in test scores between blacks and whites. Throughout the seventies black scores rose, as did whites, but the gap between black and white scores, while shrinking in size, remained. Nonetheless, generally low scores of both blacks and whites supported critics who had questioned the academic quality of American schools. Many of these critics now opposed the changes, particularly busing children to distant neighborhoods, intended to produce equal educational opportunity.

Lurking in the background of the debate about improving schools for the poor was the role of education in the American democracy. Did everyone need to achieve academically or only some? How much knowledge did we all need? How much virtue did the society require from us? Would eliminating racial segregation by law increase civic virtue? Did the poor get as good an education in school as the rich, and if not, was that fair? How should we decide where to focus our educational resources?

The policy that led to the creation in 1964 of Head Start, a publicly funded preschool program for low-income children, illustrated this dilemma. It was intended to enable those youngsters to do better academically in school and subsequently in life than similarly situated four-year-olds without the program. Did it? Since only a minority of the eligible children was enrolled and little attention was given to the quality of the programs themselves, this was not an easy question to answer for the many evaluation experts who hedged their replies by correctly pointing to inadequate information.

Beginning in 1962 with 123 low-income three- and four-year-olds, in an effort with goals similar to Head Start, David Weikart and his colleagues at the Perry PreSchool Project in Ypsilanti, Michigan, placed half the children in identifiably strong preschool programs and the other half in none, and followed them for forty years. Not surprisingly, but providing great relief to the researchers, those who attended the preschool did much better in life than those who did not. Weikart could also put numbers on his preschool program: $15,000 in inflation-adjusted dollars spent on each child saved $145,000 in potential welfare, prison, and other public expenditures for the others. More important, he explained what the fundamental constituent elements of his program were. Presumably without full implementation of those elements, including well-paid teachers who made weekly home visits, the results would have been less successful. Most evaluations of preschool programs fail to pay attention to salary levels or the quality of home visits, thus omitting indicators that may be critical to the effectiveness of the program.

Congress, which was spending considerable sums on Title I of the Elementary and Secondary Education Act, naturally sought an evaluation of its efforts. Not until the 1978 National Institute of Education study, led by Paul Hill and Iris Rotberg, was there much credible evidence about its effect. Even in that comprehensive study the focus was upon what Congress had intended: namely had the money gone to the places it was supposed to go, had it purchased the services intended, and had the services reached the eligible students. In short, the access issues were primary. Only in one report was there much discussion of any gains in academic achievement that could be traced to the legislation. In it the researchers found that in well-managed Title I programs (and by no means were all well managed) students made gains in reading and arithmetic. The evaluation experts found it easier to trace the money and the students receiving services than they did to explain what constituted "well managed." That conundrum did not fit their research designs, yet it was key to explaining the success of the program.

CHANGING POLITICAL EMPHASES

Because federal officials were so influential in enunciating what Americans wanted from education in the period from 1954 to 1983, what happened politically in Washington had profound ramifications for education, much more than in most previous periods. Therefore, the election of Richard Nixon in 1968, bringing with it the opportunity for Republicans to appoint new Supreme Court justices, had a major impact on the public schools. Nixon appointed four new members of the Supreme Court, including William Rehnquist, thus creating a shift in the majority of the Court. The new Court did not pursue desegregation with the same vigor as the Warren Court.

With the new Court appointees essentially the steam went out of the federal government's efforts to achieve "equal educational opportunity." The 1973 five-to-four decision, *San Antonio* v. *Rodriguez*, heralded the change in the federal support for equal educational opportunity. The Mexican Americans lost their case seeking federal help in forcing Texas to provide funds for their schools comparable to funds for other nearby but better-funded schools, thus demonstrating the shift in the Nixon Court. In 1974 the Court decided, again by a five-to-four majority, in *Milliken* v. *Bradley* that busing across city lines (in this case, Detroit) was not necessary to achieve desegregation. This decision preserved suburbs as potential racial refuges. Nixon's attention to his Watergate difficulties after 1972 probably prevented his taking more substantive political action to limit desegregation.

Despite Nixon's inattention to schooling issues, northern communities increasingly found themselves under federal district court pressure to change enrollment patterns so that more black and white children could become classmates. Again, the issue was "access" to classrooms previously out of reach. When ordered by the courts, school administrators and teachers attempted to follow the law, but quieting the attendant disruptions took much of their energy, and not much time or effort was left for instruction. J. Anthony Lukas revealed these pressures in his *Common Ground*, a particularly graphic description of the turmoil in Boston following Judge Arthur Garrity's 1974 order to mix black and white high school students in South Boston and Charlestown. In the wake of such conflict, simply making the schools safe was a major undertaking. Again, the children were being expected to accomplish what most adults of different races had failed to do: work together efficiently in the same space.

Race was not the only issue that triggered educational debate. So did language. In the American Southwest many people had traditionally spoken their family language, Spanish, sometimes for several generations of residence in the United States. When these children entered school, if they did, they encountered an environment in which many found their ability to succeed limited. Dropout rates were high and college admission low. The Bilingual Education Act of 1968 provided limited federal funds to support these children's education. The 1974 *Lau* v. *Nichols* Supreme Court decision, which concluded that "equality of treatment" was not possible for children without English facility where the instructional language was English, supplemented the 1968 act. School districts struggled to find instructional accommodations for these students. Many conflicting evaluations later, half of the states required assistance for these children but did not specify the kind of program necessary for them. Twenty-five years ago the political support for "maintenance" of the family language, rather than "transition" to English, was considerable, particularly among Hispanics. Many immigrants who came to the United States during the dramatic influx of the eighties and nineties, however, came expecting to learn English in addition to their family languages, such as Vietnamese, Farsi, or Russian. Attention has shifted to the means by which these children can become fluent in English, without denigrating their native language or family culture. While many such youngsters have difficulty, nonetheless, the rolls of high school valedictorians now include many seniors who have managed this "transition," just as little Victor did.

Another group of advocates was working the Washington scene in the 1970s: these were the activists for children with disabilities. Under the rubric of "equal educational opportunity" these individuals, often parents of such children, sought "mainstreaming" to keep their offspring in regular classrooms, rather in special schools or classes. The "access" they sought was for their children to participate not in "special education" programs but in the regular classes, albeit with some additional arrangements, including an individual education plan (IEP) that outlined the particular accommodations to be made for that student. Unlike desegregation, in which issues of both race and class clouded the discussion, persons seeking "inclusion" for children with disabilities came from all social and racial groups, including very powerful and affluent ones, such as families of members of Congress. Problems of physical, mental, or emotional disability affected many, many families, and they formed extraordinarily effective lobbying groups for both research and action for their needs. As a consequence, the Education for All Handicapped Children Act passed in 1975, and by the 1978–1979 school year the public schools were required to become "fully responsible for the free and appropriate education of handicapped persons, aged 3 to 18." This mandate was laid upon the schools as enrollments were in sharp decline, and states such as California and Massachusetts were passing legislation reducing school funding.

Finally, in 1977, bad news about U.S. schools came from former secretary of labor Willard Wirtz, who led a panel that attempted to explain to a skeptical public why scores on college admission tests, specifically the Scholastic Aptitude Test (SAT), had declined precipitously over the prior two decades. These scores reflected the academic achievement not only of the gifted and talented but also of the rank-and-file students, still wallowing in the life adjustment curriculum. The panel explained that the decline resulted, in part, from the dramatic increase in the number of students taking the test during this period, many of whom were not as strong academically as the select group to whom the test was previously limited. The other half of their explanation was largely an assortment of cultural factors that collectively led to adolescents' diminished interest in education. In a separate paper prepared for the panel, reading expert Jeanne Chall suggested that perhaps the students were not being taught well and were not spending enough time in school on academic material. In the plethora of policy explanations, this wise voice was nearly lost.

WHAT AMERICANS THOUGHT

And what did the American public make of all this? First of all, they complained. They did not like busing, though many fewer children spent time on buses for desegregation than were bused to consolidated schools in rural areas. Many Americans were unhappy about bilingual education, though that controversy faded. Despite these dissatisfactions, they kept their children in the public schools. In 1960, for example, 86 percent of American schoolchildren attended public schools while about 13 percent attended Roman Catholic schools, and the rest were distributed among various private schools, both religious and secular. By 1983 the percent of children in public schools had increased to 87 percent, but the Roman Catholic school enrollment had dropped to 7 percent with an increase in enrollment in other private schools. But Americans, both parents and the increasing numbers of Americans who did not have school-age children, were increasingly critical of the schools in general and even of their own schools. In 1974, 69 percent gave their local public schools a grade of A, B, or C, but by 1981 only 63 percent did, with a big drop in the As and an increase in the Cs.

Americans have always ranked the nation's schools lower than their local ones, but their commitment to the schools themselves seemed to diminish. In 1969, 75 percent of Americans would have liked a child of theirs to teach in a public school, while 15 percent would not. By 1981 only 46 percent would favor such a choice and 43 percent would not, a factor undoubtedly affected by the growing vocational opportunities for women in this period. On the two major federal education initiatives, desegregation and Title I, the public in the early 1980s seemed to concur, with 89 percent indicating that whites and blacks should be able to attend the same schools and 71 percent believing Title I was effective. In short, the principles and perhaps even the policies seemed right for a democracy that valued fairness for all its citizens, but the practices were worrisome.

Ronald Reagan was elected president and came to Washington in 1981 promising to eliminate the U.S. Department of Education, which had just been created at the end of the Carter administration. Pundits charged that it was a payoff to the National Education Association for its support of Jimmy Carter in the 1976 presidential election and anticipated support in 1980.

Whether the creation of the department was, in fact, beneficial for American education is indeed debatable. For the many teachers and administrators, however, who had been laboring in the public schools for the past twenty-five years or so, Reagan's proposal to eliminate it seemed simply another example of the denigration of their work and effort. For adults working in schools it seemed further evidence that the public wanted schools to solve the social problems that families, communities, and the government were not able, or willing, to address themselves.

Having been buffeted by rapidly expanding and then declining enrollments, by the blizzard of curriculum reform for the academically able in the fifties and sixties, by the overwhelming trauma of racism that infused the arguments about desegregation, by the difficulties of bringing low-income students to the same academic level as affluent ones, and finally by the increasing bureaucratization and loss of public confidence in their enterprise, teachers and administrators understandably were exhausted. Thus far, they had dealt with most of these problems by following the directives of outsiders—academics, bureaucrats, and judges—providing access to special programs in order to equalize educational opportunity. Their enterprise lacked coherence. Tinkering around the edges left a void in the center.

Dissatisfaction with traditional schooling was growing. Adolescent culture was being overtaken by media, consumerism, and other sources of immediate gratification that were inimical to sustained schoolwork. Professional expertise had concentrated on developing special programs, not on improving regular classes. Soon reliance upon special programs would prove insufficient, and pressure would come to improve the regular programs. "All children can learn" ran the rhetoric, but whether all schools could teach them satisfactorily remained to be seen.

FOUR

———————

Achievement
1983-Present

Milton Goldberg worried. As he entered the White House State Dining Room with the members of the commission that he had staffed for the previous two years, the teacher and administrator from Philadelphia pondered what the president of the United States, Ronald Reagan, would say about the report on which they had labored so vigorously. Everyone understood that most federal commission documents descend into immediate obscurity. He feared that destiny for their report. He also feared that the president would call again for policies, such as prayer in schools, vouchers for private school tuition, tuition tax credits, or abolition of the Department of Education (Goldberg's current employer), that the commission had not endorsed.

The president strode vigorously into the room as Goldberg rose anxiously. Reagan genially introduced the report, saying that it fully accorded with his earlier enunciated views on education. Obviously he had not read the report since it did not deal with any of those issues. This report was Reagan's last major presidential effort on education, although he continued to discuss education in various speeches.

The commissioners, who sought public attention for their report as a stimulus to change, feared that the press would now ignore the report, believing they had written a Reagan-support document. As one of the commissioners, physicist Gerald Holton, reported, the authors were appalled and one said loudly enough for the press to hear, "We have been had." Hearing the remark, journalists in attendance suddenly developed an intense interest in the report. They immediately recognized a profound disconnect between the Reagan administration's rhetoric about education and the content of the report. Both the political disconnect and the subject matter initially intrigued them, but the substance of

President Ronald Reagan (center left) welcomed the panel that prepared *A Nation at Risk*, including Secretary of Education Terrel Bell on Reagan's right, Chairman David Gardner on Reagan's left and Staff Director Milton Goldberg, seated at far rear right. *Courtesy of Milton Goldberg*

the document caught the public's attention and has remained there for nearly a quarter of a century.

A Nation at Risk alerted the American people, often in rather colorful and occasionally purple and erroneous prose, to the danger the country faced if the academic achievement of schoolchildren did not improve. The commissioners opined, "If an unfriendly foreign power had attempted to impose on America the mediocre educational performance that exists today, we might well have viewed it as an act of war."

Assertions that the United States was committing unilateral disarmament by failing to educate its children or that American youth were less well educated than their parents, caught the imagination, if not the intellect, of Americans. At the beginning, that was what the report's advocates and foes remembered and discussed, not the report's sensible, moderate suggestions for a strong academic curriculum in the high school, higher retention rates in schools and colleges, adequate financial investment in education, supplementary federal support of local and state school districts, or voluntary efforts to strengthen education programs. Initially no one mentioned these findings much. The report also continued, "Our concern, however, goes well beyond matters such as industry and commerce. It also includes the intellectual, moral, and spiritual strengths of our people which knit together the very fabric of our society. . . . A high level of shared education is essential to a free, democratic society." Few commentators on the report noted that section either.

While much of the rhetoric was wildly overblown, including images of a "declaration of war" and citations of dubious research about prior levels of educational achievement in the United States, James Harvey, a staff member at the National Institute of Education, provided one tellingly accurate phrase, "the rising tide of mediocrity" sweeping the schools. During the access era, in which new programs were being devised but little attention was given to their effectiveness, such a tide was understandable. Access had focused not on improving the academic quality of schooling in general but rather providing special programs for those with particular needs. Many such programs emerged, but strong academic programs for everyone had not been on the agenda. The core experiences of many American schools, particularly those serving middle- and working-class children, which included most minority and, once again, immigrant youth, were vestiges of the adjustment era. A rigorous academic curriculum was available only to a few, as the life adjustment enthusiasts had deemed appropriate, and most of the students encountered a school experience replete with driver's training, health and safety, and academic courses with low expectations. The life that those courses prepared one for was one of extraordinarily limited skills, and such skills did not command jobs with decent wages in the eighties.

The genesis of *A Nation at Risk,* however, came not from educational dilemmas, but from political necessity. The politically gifted actor Ronald Reagan had come to the presidency in 1981, the day the Iranians released the American hostages, and on that note of hope he began his first term, a profound stylistic contrast to the sometimes dour but always conscientious and committed President Carter. One of Reagan's campaign promises, to eliminate the new U.S. Department of Education, could not be immediately fulfilled. Therefore, he had to appoint a secretary of education, and he persuaded former commissioner of the U.S. Office of Education Terrel Bell to become the "thirteenth man" in his cabinet.

Reluctantly Bell drove a U-Haul truck with his household goods from Salt Lake City to Washington, considering his assignment to preside over a department set for elimination. While frontal attack was inappropriate, Bell concluded that a national commission reporting on the state of education in America might be a good—perhaps final—task for the department. He got his Utah neighbor, David Gardner, to chair it and assembled a mix of politically appropriate persons to serve. Since the group wanted a name that would invoke public support but not commit them to a specific agenda, they termed themselves the Commission on Excellence in Education. The commissioners included some representatives of the public, an assortment of schoolteachers and administrators, and, harking back to the days of scientists developing school curricula, two distinguished physicists. Bell recommended Milton Goldberg, whom Gardner confirmed, to gather a staff drawn heavily from the National Institute of Education (soon to be eliminated by the Reagan administration).

Having first worried that the report would be lost, Goldberg now found that the astonishing public reception nearly took over his life with demands for travel and speeches throughout the country. The articulate, engaging, and jocular educator found himself reviled by some former colleagues for criticisms in the report that they found too extreme and endorsed by other individuals who expected the schools immediately to convert reluctant scholars into academic powerhouses, a highly unlikely scenario. From his years of experience as an educator, Goldberg understood that neither the critique nor the support was fully justified. What the report sought, high levels of academic achievement for everybody, was unlikely to occur soon.

Goldberg remembered vividly and fondly the years he had spent in Philadelphia public schools laboring to increase equality of educational opportunity, the dominant goal in the access era. He had worked hard to achieve this with the predominantly low-income children he served. To him the fundamental thrust of *A Nation at Risk*, if not its rhetoric, was consistent with the priorities of the earlier era. But initially the rhetoric, not the recommendations, caught the public's attention.

DEMISE OF EQUAL EDUCATIONAL OPPORTUNITY

Why did equal educational opportunity fall so swiftly from public attention, Goldberg and many others similarly committed to its message of fairness and improvement wondered? Utterly consistent with democracy, few could fault it as a desirable end. But as the embodiment of a policy, many challenged it, particularly when its implementation altered practice in their neighborhoods, as it did with school desegregation, Title I programs, bilingual classes, mainstreaming of children with disabilities, and the provision of sports programs for girls equal with those of boys.

One important aspect of the criticism of equal educational opportunity was the anger many whites either expressed openly or felt silently at the notion that their children would have to attend schools with blacks. As blacks watched desegregation efforts, not all of them thought they were an improvement for their children either. Many of the schools undergoing desegregation either as a result of court orders or under voluntary plans were considerably disrupted in the process, thus limiting the educational activities that could occur. Probably the greatest loss was the changing ambiance of schools. Increasing bureaucratization of these institutions, beginning in the late sixties, came as federal money began trickling into districts, requiring accurate accounting of its expenditure on the federal priorities. At the same time school violence increased until the mid-1970s when it leveled off and increased again in the early 1980s. Uniformed guards became widespread in big city schools, as those communities experienced riots in the same period. By 1994 the federal government began requiring school safety programs, which prompted the proliferation of metal detectors. Crime in neighborhoods affected life in schools. Family instability made schooling of children more difficult, and there was plenty of instability as divorce rates rose and out-of-wedlock babies arrived. Drug and alcohol use increased first among high school and then middle school students, creating more difficult conditions for learning.

These changes dramatically altered the warm and comforting school environment familiar to the readers of *Dick and Jane* to one in which hostility was evident. I recall sitting in a teachers' room in a New York City junior high school during those years and hearing the white teachers routinely refer to the students, most of whom were black or Hispanic, as "animals." That was not an environment that was conducive to learning. It is hard to imagine that any parents would choose to have their child in such a situation.

American schooling in the seventies presented a problem in which the link between policy and practice was tenuous at best. The goal of the policy, equal educational opportunity, was admirable. Making it happen was very difficult. One element of the difficulty was the relationship between opportunity and results. Efforts, undoubtedly inadequate, to provide equal opportunity failed to provide equal results. Disparity in results was much more evident than genuine equality of opportunity. In fact, dissatisfaction with the academic performance of most American children became the national political issue that *A Nation at Risk* highlighted. Americans woke up to the fact that many of their children, particularly ones of color, had not mastered academic subjects. These were precisely the children who were now being expected to lead in the desegregation of the schools, joining previously all-white classrooms. Evidence rapidly mounted that many of the white children lacked academic skills as well.

For many Americans who did not want to be called racist, it seemed easier to fight for greater academic achievement, a goal that few would dispute, than to deal with disparities in opportunity between blacks and whites, rich and poor directly. If the child failed to achieve, the blame could rest either with the child or the school, and Americans could conveniently ignore the profoundly different cultural resources affecting wealthy white children and poor black ones.

During all the previous decades of American schools "results," defined as measurable academic achievement, had not been a primary educational goal for most children. Basic literacy was expected of all, but, as high schools demonstrated, not much else was required for graduation. Achieving academically had always been the goal for a few, including those living in poverty and those of color, as well as those who expected or whose parents expected them to attend an academically demanding college and for some who simply found academic study congenial to their talent and temperament. But it was not an expectation that was applied to all students.

When the emphasis was upon access, the principal effort had been to help students participate in educational programs that previously had not been available to them. The quality or effectiveness of these programs in increasing academic achievement for all participants was rarely the focus. In the thirty years when the goal had been adjustment, primary attention had been on meeting the psychosocial needs of youngsters and helping them fit into their expected niche in society. Again, academic achievement for some was always valued, but not for everybody. At the beginning of the century, when assimilation was a main goal of the schools, helping children become Americans did not mean academic achievement. It meant some English language facility but, more important, a broad cultural acceptance of values embodied in this society. Each of these goals had genuine value and benefit both to the student and to the society, but each carried to an extreme led to difficulties that caused reappraisal of the schools' role in the nation.

Throughout American history our democratic society has required citizens to possess both virtue and knowledge, generally in that order of priority. Enthusiasm for *A Nation at Risk* reversed those priorities, primarily because many Americans feared that our economy was falling behind that of other nations whose citizens were more proficient academically than ours. Better schooling, they thought, would help. Few wished to consider "the limits of schooling," as Christopher Jencks had hoped to entitle his book *Inequality*.

AMERICAN AMBIVALENCE TOWARD ACADEMIC ACHIEVEMENT

As Richard Hofstadter wrote wisely many decades ago in *Anti-Intellectualism in American Life*, Americans have an unease bordering on antipathy toward intellectuals, and this attitude has shaped our view of academic achievement. Few individuals were of higher status in American life than the 1920s Princeton undergraduate who eschewed serious study, took pride in his "gentleman's C," and whom F. Scott Fitzgerald chronicled in his novels. This fellow and others like him enjoyed the social prestige of a famous college but neither he nor many of his professors engaged in rigorous academic work, and nobody faulted them. Academic excellence was not widely sought.

The traits that Americans have consistently valued are initiative, ingenuity, integrity, teamwork, and hard work. They have served us well. America became a world power in the mid-twentieth century when its population had been educated under the rubrics of assimilation and adjustment and with those American cultural values. These qualities are some distance from the contemporary measure of academic achievement: answers to tests.

Reassessment of goals for the public schools was in the air in the late 1970s and early 1980s. Fostered by Republican administrations for all but four of the two dozen years between 1968 and 1992, the tide of public sentiment turned toward regarding schooling primarily as preparation for employment, not citizenship. Many Americans, including Nixon and Reagan appointees to the Supreme Court, found the access commitments, particularly as they applied to desegregation of the public schools, had gone too far. While few still believed that blacks should be prohibited by law from attending schools with whites, many preferred that the law permit such desegregation but that their own school not engage in it to any significant degree. Living in a racially segregated community, and such communities were increasing in numbers, was the best means of avoiding desegregation, a fact that became evident after the Supreme Court's *Milliken* decision declared that desegregation plans of city schools need not include suburbs.

Soon decisions in Oklahoma City and Kansas City cases in the 1980s marked a change in the Court's interpretation of constitutional requirements, as plans intended to foster greater desegregation of schoolchildren by race in those communities were rejected. Whether this was simply a different reading of the law or a manifestation of judicial activism in which the new majority of justices sought outcomes consistent with their political views remains a matter of heated debate. There was no debate, however, about whether American children, particularly those in the inner city, needed stronger academic skills at the end of the twentieth century. Typically the argument was expressed in terms of jobs that required these abilities, not the needs of the democracy for enlightened citizens.

Gradually Americans realized that educational results were badly skewed, as the researchers had already explained. Middle- and upper-class Americans generally scored higher on academic achievement tests and others typically scored lower. On average, whites scored higher than blacks or Hispanics but lower than Asians in mathematics. There were important exceptions, of course, but the pattern held just as James Coleman, Christopher Jencks, and others had described. These differential scores were not new, and they did not result from the equal educational opportunity initiatives. Rather, they were a consequence of long-term patterns in many communities that had not placed a high value on academic achievement. Schools themselves had contributed to these differences, reinforcing them in most cases with the least prepared teachers going to the schools with the lowest performing students while the best prepared, more experienced teachers went to the highest performing students. But schooling was not the primary explanation for the academic disparities. Rather, the differences were primarily those of social class but manifest to Americans as rural versus urban or South versus North, as well as black versus white. Because for the first half of the twentieth century blacks were concentrated in the rural South, a region of limited educational opportunities, the generally low academic performance was not surprising to whites and especially not to blacks.

Perhaps the biggest change in the public schools came in the cities, which had been considered to have the best schools in the nation during the first half of the century. After World War II dramatic population shifts occurred as middle- and upper-class families, most of whom were white, moved to the suburbs. The federal government facilitated these moves through low mortgage rates and subsidies for new commuter highways. As a result, by the latter years of the twentieth century the largest city school districts served primarily low-income minority students. Thus, when the federal government retreated in the 1980s from insisting upon equal educational opportunity it was reinforcing the resegregation by race and by social class that was occurring in the schools. Concentrations of unemployed adults and their offspring populated many inner cities, as William Julius Wilson described in *When Work Disappears.* Such communities were not in a position to demand or to get good schools for their needy children.

DETERMINING WHAT AMERICANS KNOW

During most of the twentieth century, Americans had not paid very much public attention to quantitative measures of academic achievement. Students selected for "gifted and talented" classes were usually chosen based on multiple measures, including teacher recommendations, not test scores alone. For all the years of entrancement with IQs, children's individual scores were supposed to be secret or only shared with teachers and occasionally parents. Unlike Britain, America did not require school-leaving exams to determine whether a student could continue in school. Rather, we treated school completion as a process, as in, "Did you pass enough courses to graduate?"

Until the National Assessment of Educational Progress (NAEP), a federal testing program to assess the competence of American youth in various academic subjects, began in 1969 and gradually accumulated data over time, Americans had no widespread indicators of academic achievement that could be identified by race, gender, or even locale. Initially, local and state education officials refused to administer the tests if the results were to be reported in their jurisdictions. Americans, including the many with segregated school systems, preferred not to know how inadequate the overall results were. With NAEP initially reporting by age, race, gender, and region, scores became available, and they were not heartening for anybody. Generally, seventeen-year-old black students scored about the same in reading and mathematics as thirteen-year-old whites. Nor were these results surprising to well-informed educators. But until these results became public, as the federal intervention made possible, action to improve education for blacks was limited. However, the best evidence reveals that academic achievement for southern blacks was rising steadily in the latter decades of the twentieth century, but their achievement was still substantially below whites, and average white scores did not bring much pride either. Should a democracy permit both such low mean scores and such race-identifiable educational gaps to continue?

Few defended either white or black American students' academic performance. If there was anything about education with which there was agreement, it was that more academic achievement was a good idea for everybody. Just as the curriculum of assimilation was considered beneficial to the immigrant as well as the native born, so the enthusiasts of achievement believed it to be good for all. In fact, the academic performance of students in America's best high schools and of some in much less demanding schools had been and continued to be remarkably good, as evidenced by students' performance on various national competitions—such as National Merit or Westinghouse Science—and by their subsequent academic performance in demanding colleges.

The public conversation about education after 1983 focused on the economic rewards of education. In that respect, *A Nation at Risk* was the most recent major statement of why education was necessary for the nation. The national discussion about education soon shifted to why education was good for economic growth and for my child's financial success. News that male college graduates made lots more money than male high school graduates, hardly surprising, flooded the media. Soon the value of education was being expressed principally in terms of how it would improve one's likelihood of getting a well-paying job. Business leaders sought a more highly educated work force capable of bringing greater productivity to their companies. The rationale for education was rapidly narrowing from one that supported education for what it could do for the nation (make better citizens) to what it could do for the company and for the individual (get and do a better job). As the purpose of schooling narrowed, so did the measure of educational quality. What counted now was one's test score.

DARKENING AMERICAN MOOD

American school children's academic performances, woeful as many believed them to be, became a metaphor for the country's mood. President Jimmy Carter had become so concerned about the national miasma that he convened a series of miniconferences at Camp David to discuss what was wrong with the country. Gas prices at the pump were at record highs, and gas was in short supply. Historian Christopher Lasch captured the national moral in his 1979 study, *A Culture of Narcissism: American Life in an Age of Diminishing Ex-*

pectations. Carter looked to a variety of American leaders to learn how the country might pull up its collective socks and recapture its legendary optimism and competence. When Iran held fifty-two Americans hostage from November 1979 to January 1981, and Carter and the U.S. government were unable to secure their release either through diplomatic or military means, it appeared to many that America really had lost its grip.

American business was also in trouble, facing powerful competition from its World War II adversaries, Germany and Japan. After their defeat and the devastation of their economies, they had restructured their companies and now seemed to be outperforming their victorious American counterparts, which had not been forced to reorganize. The U.S. stock market had been nearly stagnant throughout the 1970s, and many pundits in the early 1980s did not voice much optimism about the economy, which was encumbered by mounting deficits, inflation, and rising energy prices. Initially business leaders' explanation for their difficulties was the inadequacy of American workers, who, they claimed, were not adequately educated to perform the new tasks required of them. When American business and the U.S. economy took off in the late 1980s and 1990s, credit was given to American management's improved leadership. Workers and their poor education were blamed for failures, but management and its organizational skills got the credit for success.

A NATION AWASH IN EDUCATION REPORTS

In a nation ill at ease about its future but not in a lethal crisis, education often emerges as a focus of attention. Educate the children better so that they can solve the troublesome problems we face. In the early 1980s, the nation received a number of other reports in addition to *A Nation at Risk* with similar substantive messages: all our children need a stronger academic education. Most of these documents had begun their gestation two or three years earlier.

The Twentieth Century Fund, a progressive Manhattan think tank, organized a disparate group of educators under the leadership of Robert Wood, a political scientist active in the Johnson administration and subsequently president of the University of Massachusetts and briefly superintendent of Boston's public schools. Their 1983 report, *Making the Grade*, appeared the same week as the U.S. Department of Education's with similar conclusions but substantially less dramatic rhetoric. The National Science Board organized another commission under the leadership of the distinguished civil rights lawyer William Coleman to consider math, science, and technology education. The Committee on Economic Development, a business group, issued its report, *Action for Excellence*. Ernest Boyer, commissioner of the U.S. Office of Education in the Carter administration and now president of the Carnegie Foundation for the Advancement of Teaching, published *High School*, and found American secondary schools in need of considerable improvement. Diane Ravitch, a distinguished historian of education and a member of the Twentieth Century Fund task force, brought out a book in 1985 entitled *The Troubled Crusade, 1945–80*, which offered a severe critique of American education during that period, particularly of the academic laxity of schooling. Theodore Sizer, former head of the Harvard Graduate School of Education, Phillips Academy, Andover, and the Coalition of Essential Schools, characterized the frustration of an English teacher working in a bureaucratic setting with low academic expectations for students in *Horace's Compromise*.

Though *A Nation at Risk* received the most publicity, all these reports of the early 1980s expressed similar sentiments and reminded experienced educators of the criticisms of the early 1950s. Once again, the rhetoric called for increased academic achievement. But the principal difference was that this time the call was for academic achievement for the many, not just for a few. The reality remained that academic excellence was concentrated among the affluent few with good schools and supportive educational environments.

Bestor's and Rickover's emphasis reappeared in some of the critiques. The intensity varied, sometimes even within the same document. *Making the Grade* opened with "The nation's public schools are in trouble," and its background paper, written by the well-known political scientist and educational policy expert Paul Peterson, began, "Americans have been proud of their public educational institutions, and rightly so." Peterson's conclusion was positive but alerted readers to emerging problems, particularly academic performances of high school students in mathematics and science: "The crisis in American education is greatly exaggerated," Peterson wrote. He continued:

> For decades the American educational system has flourished. . . . Schools were valued as one of the few public institutions that were part of every community, that reached all classes and races, that combined a sensitivity to regional and local differences with a capacity to provide a relatively standard set of services, and that symbolized the nation's democratic ideal of equal opportunity and citizen responsibility.

By 2003, twenty years after its publication, Peterson concluded, the problems were much more severe.

The ambivalence about how good or bad the schools really were undoubtedly reflected the conviction that access alone was not enough. Parents, whose children were the schools' consumers (or "customers" as the current faddish business terminology dictated), wanted not just a program for their child but also some evidence that the child was benefiting from the program. Many parents believed that local programs were providing benefits but were dubious about the success of programs nationally. Their skepticism was well placed, particularly in the high schools, but in many elementary schools as well.

Perhaps the book which best captured the national educational dilemma was Arthur Powell, Eleanor Farrar, and David K. Cohen's 1985 volume, *The Shopping Mall High School*, whose title embraced youths' primary commitment to consumerism, which coexisted in tension with their school attendance requirement. It illustrated the power these youth had to resist instruction and also revealed the accommodations school personnel made when faced with this resistance, such as reducing the academic demands of schooling. Students who took time-consuming after-school jobs and who had no time or inclination to study sought and found less demanding schoolwork. This tacit agreement reached by teachers and administrators did not challenge the students' preference for money over study. In short, students were required by compulsory attendance laws and sometimes by their parents to show up at school, but they were not required to study or learn.

All these reports and analyses were long on what troubled schools, short on how to improve them. Conservatives favored policy solutions involving private schools, which they asserted were superior to public ones. They failed, however, to explain why, besides the participation of more children from well-educated and affluent families who brought with them greater "social capital," such institutions were superior. Simplistic solutions, such as requiring school uniforms, or unrealistic ones, such as getting rid of the teachers unions, abounded. Few dealt with the fundamental issue of taking children from families without much education or many social supports and, through the relatively weak intervention of schooling, converting their expectations and accomplishments to those typical of successful middle-class children.

The schools serving inner-city youth, now primarily children of color, had weak records of academic achievement, with the exception of a few students. The protracted years of dispute over desegregation, particularly in northern cities, had left many of those schools bereft of middle-class parents, both white and black, who were the stalwart supporters of education in most communities. The presence of such concerned parents may well have been simply a marker indicating the broader community's commitment to its schools and its youth in many varied ways. Schools function best when their values and those of the students' families and the community are in close alignment. When community leaders attribute their success to their education, then support for schools is more likely. Most inner-city schools were not situated in such communities.

ALBERT SHANKER, UNLIKELY CENTRIST

If Lucy Sprague Mitchell, the private school innovator, and Carleton Washburne, the successful Winnetka school superintendent, epitomized the adjustment era, and Francis Keppel and Harold Howe II the access period, then Albert Shanker exemplified the achievement era. Speaking incisively in a variety of public settings about the academic inadequacies of many schools, particularly urban ones, Shanker astonished the public, who had previously known him only as an aggressive defender of teachers while head of the New York City

Albert Shanker, former head of the American Federation of
Teachers, influential union leader, and broker between the
business and education communities, salutes the flag at the AFT
convention on July 4, 1988. *Photo by Russ Curtis/©American
Federation of Teachers, AFL-CIO*

Teachers Union and then the national American Federation of Teachers. Improving schools, Shanker was
fond of saying was "a heavy lift."

Shanker came from an eastern European Jewish immigrant family and had found academic success himself as a gifted student in the New York City public
schools, graduating from prestigious Stuyvesant High
School and then venturing to the University of Illinois
for a bachelor's degree. He returned to New York City
to pursue a philosophy doctorate in John Dewey's old
department at Columbia. Like Doc Howe, he did not
complete his degree, also dropping out of Columbia to
support his wife and new baby as a teacher in a New
York City junior high school.

Shanker's political and intellectual trajectory was steep. He soon moved from his mathematics classroom to work with the weakened Teachers Guild, which John Dewey had helped organize in 1915, incorporating civil rights activities, including the Selma-to-Montgomery march in spring 1965 with his fight to unionize New York City teachers. In fall 1968, he led his union in a strike that closed the New York City schools (an action for which he subsequently went to prison) in a dispute over transferring mostly white teachers out of the community-controlled, predominantly black district of Ocean Hill–Brownsville to other New York City schools. By the 1970s, Shanker was a profoundly controversial figure. He deeply believed that the public schools had been and must continue to be instruments of democracy, providing opportunity for all citizens, while at the same time he worked toward building a strong teachers union committed to active participation in both the national and international labor movement. These seemed contradictory goals to some onlookers. His verbal pyrotechnics were so well known that in his 1973 film *Sleeper*, Woody Allen named the man who destroyed the world by tossing a nuclear bomb Albert Shanker.

Although widely known to Americans, few would have guessed that Shanker would emerge as a staunch supporter of the critiques of American schools (and presumably its teachers) that had engulfed the nation for the previous quarter century. He bridged the gap between the educators and the public, particularly business and political leaders, in a way that few others managed, stressing the role of public schools in supporting democracy and therefore the crucial need for them to teach all their students effectively.

Never gifted in small talk, Shanker nonetheless had a commanding grasp of ideas and information, which he combined to great effect in his weekly columns in the *New York Times,* paid advertisements of the American Federation of Teachers that appeared in the "News of the Week in Review" section, and his many articles, formal speeches, and informal but rigorous participation in countless committees, boards, and other meetings. In the late 1980s, he joined, on a part-time basis, the faculty of the Harvard Graduate School of Education, where he had an office down the hall from Howe and Keppel. For the five years he taught, his students were treated to pungent discussions of why school reform was essential for the nation and why it was hard, and penetrating observations on how it might be accomplished. Shanker died in 1997, seven years after Keppel and five years before Howe, a trio diverse in backgrounds but united in understanding the American democracy's need for strong public schools. All three worked assiduously and effectively to help them improve. Each of these men was enormously more worldly than the Midwestern educators of the prior generation in their understanding of the complex factors that affect children's inclination and ability to learn and the school environment that enhances both.

AMERICANS' CHANGING VIEWS OF THEIR SCHOOLS

Getting a genuine understanding of what Americans thought about their schools in the 1980s is difficult as the press was filled with critiques of their academic quality. The 1983 Gallup poll revealed that most Americans believed that a lack of discipline was the schools' biggest problem, while the press was reporting their academic inadequacy. Nonetheless, the following year Gallup found public confidence in the schools the highest in a decade.

Teachers, however, had different concerns. The 1984 Gallup poll reported that teachers found parental indifference their major concern followed by limited financial support, lack of student interest, overcrowded classrooms, and discipline. Presumably the teachers felt the heat of criticism and explained lack of student academic success on nonschool factors. The same year the poll found that public confidence in the schools had risen 11 percent and that 42 percent of the respondents believed the schools were getting better. Reality was elusive.

A decade later, the 1996 poll data remained consistent with 43 percent of respondents giving their local public schools a grade of either an A or B while their opinion of schools nationally was lower. Those participating in the polls did not seem to be focused on mastery of academic subjects. The issues facing schools that they identified in 1996 (drugs, discipline, violence, gangs, and inadequate funding) were, in fact, problems rooted in families and communities, not ones created in schools, though the teachers and administrators certainly had to grapple with them. If the major problems were drugs and gangs, then it was hardly surprising that academic achievement in core subjects, such as math, English, or science, was often weak.

While the public may have been supportive of their local but not the nation's schools, the "chattering classes," as exemplified by educators, journalists, and "opinion makers," were not. Business leaders joined this group, arguing that the nation's health (and often their company's) depended on a more productive and, therefore, better educated workforce.

EXCELLENCE FOR ALL

"Excellence," a word borrowed from the name of the group that produced *A Nation at Risk* (the Commission on Excellence in Education), became the term du jour. "Excellence" was to be achieved by all. But how? The means by which such a transformation was to be reached was not clear. "Restructuring" was the first answer, followed by "systemic reform," one term as meaningless as the other. Policies seemed to be the answer, but policies do not change practice automatically, quickly, or—often—even as intended. Since the 1980s the dilemma of American educators has been how to respond to the pundits' cry to make academic achievement more widespread.

The movement for academic achievement for everybody is by far the most radical and difficult of all the educational efforts of the twentieth century. Other goals required organizational changes in the school, such as desegregating buildings or establishing separate programs for gifted students. Adjustment, not at its best but at its most common, simply meant engaging in activities that were pleasing to the child, always an easier task than forcing the child to engage in activities, such as mastering quadratic equations, that might not be congenial. Even assimilation was easier than universal excellence because, first, children who did not like it did not stay in school past the primary grades, and second, the usefulness of facility in English and familiarity with U.S. culture was evident to nearly all.

The narrow focus on academic achievement has coincided with a narrowing of people's belief in the purpose of schooling in America. As Marvin Lazerson and Norton Grubb argue in *The Education Gospel*, education increasingly is justified for its ability to enhance individual financial success, rather than its broader rationale of building a society that will benefit more of its citizens.

During the soaring stock market and the lucrative corporate mergers of the late 1980s and 1990s, lots of money became concentrated in the hands of relatively few. These few were able to secure for their children outstanding educational opportunities, either in private schools or by acquiring homes in communities with superb public schools. Sometimes, they achieved their ends through large contributions to private schools in order to assure their children's acceptance. In one such case, a financial analyst praised certain stocks inappropriately. This action triggered gifts from the appreciative company to the preschool of his choice, enabling his children's admission. In short, the powerful in the society were able to provide a panoply of excellent educational venues for their sons and daughters. While this had always been true, now it was more telling as individuals without good educations would have much greater difficulty supporting themselves in adulthood than previously, a point nearly everyone understood. Some Americans also worried that a democracy should not have an educational system that made the rich, richer and the poor, poorer; this was bad government, which was ultimately bad for the nation.

Advocates for those in the society who did not have such private resources faced a dilemma: how could their schools become better? No one had an immediate or persuasive answer to that question.

PRIVATIZATION AS PANACEA

Initially some Reaganites believed that the president's initiatives for tuition tax credits and publicly funded vouchers for children to attend private schools, which the Excellence commission had ignored, were the solution to the nation's educational problems. The theory was that governance issues were the problem with schools, and in the conservatives' view private management was better than public. Many perceived private schools (presumably thinking primarily of places such as Phillips Academy, which is an extraordinarily good school) as inevitably better than public schools. Others recognized that some Roman Catholic schools were doing a very good job educating low-income children of color, many of whom were not Catholic.

With the enthusiasm for privatization that engulfed America in the late twentieth century, some policy advocates pressed for parents, not the public, to choose the appropriate education for their children. Such advocacy begged the question of whether only the parents, and not the nation as a whole, had a legitimate interest in the welfare of the next generation's education. Public funds for education traditionally have been justified on the basis that the education served not only the child but also the nation by preparing the coming generation of citizens and workers, thus contributing to the democracy and to the economy.

Black, low-income families with children in unsatisfactory urban public schools made a very persuasive case that the public schools were not serving their children, and they were entitled to something better. One solution has been the use of public dollars (in the form of "vouchers") to support their choice of alternative, nonpublic schools. Strong voices, particularly in the Republican Party but not limited to it, brought the concerns of these parents to the school reform debate. Thus far, despite considerable efforts at evaluation, the voucher experiments in Milwaukee, Cleveland, and Dayton (where the private schools are not as fine as Phillips Academy) have not produced compelling evidence proving the superiority of either the private or public schools in raising children's test scores in math or reading.

Choice among public schools, including charter schools, is the companion policy provision to vouchers, and Minnesota, with the first statewide choice plan, is a leader in the movement to provide options to parents and students. Charter laws vary by state, but most involve creating new, usually small, schools with public funds and without many of the bureaucratic requirements governing existing public schools. Joe Nathan, a leader in their development, sees them originating in the innovative activities of the 1960s, including civil rights and the experimental pedagogical practices associated with the "open school" movement.

What these efforts reveal—and what we knew already—is that it is difficult to make immediate, dramatic improvements in student learning in any school setting. Schooling remains an important but not comprehensive treatment for ignorance.

During this period, privatization has come to public schools in another form: entrepreneurial ventures. Faced with the stodgy bureaucracies that characterize many public agencies, including schools, some have believed that the solution lay in the energy of private entrepreneurs. Perhaps the best known of them has been Chris Whittle, who has led two major efforts: Channel One and the Edison Project. Channel One installs computer networks in schools in order to provide current events news programs—complete with advertisements for products school-age children want. School people generally want the computer facilities and are willing to take the ads in order to get them. They have had less to say about the value of the news programs. Critics, of course, object to the ads being presented to a captive audience, particularly one already too tempted by consumerism, and are dubious about the value of the news. Nonetheless, the program began in 1990 and continues in twelve thousand schools, involving one-sixth of public school students.

Even more compelling has been Whittle's effort to get districts to hire his company, Edison, to run their schools. Edison, which currently operates 157 schools serving approximately 71,000 students, one-sixth of whom are in Philadelphia, is one of several such companies that have undertaken this work, particularly in troubled cities, including Baltimore and Washington, D.C. Academic results have been mixed, and financial results worse. The idea advanced by adherents of these companies that private management is always preferable to public has thus far not been corroborated.

Improving children's learning seems less related to who manages the school and how than to what is expected of the children academically and the supports provided to help them achieve it. Neither public nor private management assures effective teaching. Nonetheless, the enthusiasm with which these privatization efforts were initially greeted, particularly in the investment community, revealed the depth of concern about both the management and performance of the public schools as well as the strength of the expectation that this intervention would make money. Policy gurus sought the easier change, management, rather than the more difficult one, the creation of schools that were instructionally effective for everyone.

Other forms of private investment, especially from foundations and individual philanthropy, entered the fray of school reform as well. Beginning in the 1980s, philanthropists extended their generosity to the schools with remarkable gifts. Perhaps the best-known contributor was Walter Annenberg, who made his initial fortune with *TV Guide*, and gave $500 million to various school districts, including $50 million each to New York City, Philadelphia, Chicago, and Los Angeles to improve their schools. The personal generosity was extraordinary, but the gift, distributed over a five-year period, was a minuscule fraction of their budgets. The John D. and Catherine T. MacArthur Foundation, which gave more than $10 million in the 1990s to the public schools in its hometown, Chicago, joined a number of the nation's largest foundations—especially

Carnegie and Pew, as well as Ford, Rockefeller, Kellogg, Mellon, Mott, and Hewlett—in supporting nationwide school reform efforts. The foundations focused their efforts on raising "standards" (generally meaning "more academic achievement"). Later, at the turn of the century, the Bill and Melinda Gates Foundation, which Bill Gates created with his Microsoft fortune, began significant support for public education, particularly for the reorganization of large high schools into smaller units. James Conant, who had argued for large high schools in the 1950s to permit enough students for advanced placement courses, presumably would have deplored this development. But, to many today at a time of increasingly bureaucratic and impersonal large city high schools with enrollments of several thousand students, it seems very promising.

A second subset of foundations arose during this period with specific agendas. One of the strengths of the United States is the multiplicity of funding sources that allow different points of view to be expressed, and many of these new groups exercised their right to support schools that upheld their ideas about education. Some criticized the older foundations for "liberal bias" in their focus on problems of the poor. Mostly a reflection of their donors' or their boards' political interests, these new foundations sought to support particular educational remedies, of which "vouchers," alternatively named "choice," was a favorite. The Lynde and Harry Bradley Foundation in Milwaukee, funded by the sale of a local company to Rockwell International (an aeronautics company), was active in supporting voucher experiments in Milwaukee and across the United States as well as researchers decrying the excesses of multiculturalism. Other family foundations with similar agendas included the Scaife enterprises, John M. Olin, Smith Richardson, and Walton Family Foundation.

These foundations and the organizations they supported—such as the American Enterprise Institute, Heritage Foundation, Manhattan Institute, Pioneer Institute, Cato Institute, and Thomas B. Fordham Foundation—gave a vital voice to the point of view that American public schools were not doing a satisfactory job and that some other arrangements, including privately based and absent teachers unions, would be a better solution to America's school dilemmas. But ideas about how this should occur remained elusive. None has yet accomplished academic improvement on a large scale, though many small positive innovations can be found. Nor has broad success yet come to the most troubled group of institutions, high schools.

New American Schools Development Corporation, supported by both federal and private funds, was an invention of the first Bush administration to develop new school organizations that would enhance students' academic achievement. They supported a variety of innovative programs ranging from traditional academics (Roots and Wings and Modern Red Schoolhouse) to curricula based on expeditionary learning, to an integration of the ideas of educational researchers James Comer, Howard Gardner, and Theodore Sizer called Project Atlas.

Perhaps the most important innovation of New American Schools was the recognition that both ideas and money were necessary to bring about these improvements. Finding enough of both was very difficult. After a decade of experimentation and a Rand Corporation evaluation reporting—at best—mixed results, many of the projects faded from view. Probably the best known of these experiments, Robert Slavin's Success for All, has persisted, particularly in low-income neighborhoods where educators used their federal funds from Title I of the Elementary and Secondary Education Act to pay for it. Many believed that its highly scripted pedagogical approach (teachers followed precisely a detailed instructional format) was beneficial for children needing structure and for teachers whose own academic skills were in doubt. What is more important but presently not clear is what the legacy will be of some of the more imaginative but currently less fashionable efforts.

PUBLIC SCHOOL REFORM EFFORTS

Despite these forays by entrepreneurs and foundations, the center of the debates about improving academic achievement for American youth has been the public schools themselves, which currently enroll 89 percent of our schoolchildren. State governments and local communities, which together fund more than 90 percent of school expenses, have demonstrated that they understand they are supposed to increase academic achievement in their schools.

David Hornbeck, then state superintendent of public instruction in Maryland and head of the Chief State School Officers, convened his fellow "chiefs" in Montana for their annual summer meeting in 1987. These educational leaders heard from various academic researchers about how "all children can learn" and how schools must change to make this happen. The speakers were much stronger on their convictions about children's capacities to learn and the social constraints currently preventing them from doing so than they were on what transformations must occur in the schools to enable the youngsters to gain academic mastery. Presumably the culture of the school needed to change to embrace this vision, and teachers, whose inadequacies many identified as a source of the problem, must become not the source of but the solution to the problem. The chiefs listened attentively but pondered whether the constraints illuminated in detail by the speakers were amenable to remedy by the state governments they represented.

State governments soon emerged as the principal force for reform, largely because of the national hesitation to have the federal government move into direct involvement with school practice and curriculum, which, heretofore, had been state and local prerogatives. Republican administrations under Reagan and George H. W. Bush were particularly sensitive to the tradition of local and state control of schools. Neither did Democratic president Bill Clinton, who had risen politically through state government in Arkansas, want to invoke the heavy hand of the federal government, associated as it had been with such politically sensitive issues as desegregation through the Office of Civil Rights. Thus, center stage for educational reform moved from the federal government, which had led changes in the access era, to the states.

Both presidents Bush and Clinton convened various summits with governors and their chief education officers. These meetings set goals, a politically congenial task for the different branches of government. Probably the most utopian was for U.S. students to be first in the world in mathematics in 2000. American students languished in the middle of the pack of developed countries in mathematical achievement. Because more than half of their science teachers and nearly half of the math teachers had not majored in their teaching areas, this goal seemed extremely unlikely, and, in fact, it was not reached. In schools serving low-income students, the fraction of math and science teachers who had majored in these subjects was even lower. The scores of these students, not surprisingly, were also much lower than were the scores of affluent children, who were also more likely to have teachers well prepared in math and science. Such disparities reflect the distance between an aspiration or hope for schooling and the reality faced by children who suffer the consequences of inadequate instruction from teachers who are ill-equipped to instruct them.

STANDARDS AS THE SOLUTION

By the late 1990s school reform advocates had dismissed "restructuring," "systemic reform," and even "goals" as these battle cries were replaced with "standards." This last term of art translates somewhat better into practice than its predecessors since it, in fact, defines what a teacher should instruct the students and what they should learn. Whether the teacher is effective and whether the pupils learn is another matter, but the assumption is that the tests that students must now pass to progress will be based on the standards. Sometimes they are, sometimes not.

Some unit of government, not the federal government but states or localities, began in the 1990s to set these standards and require that all students meet them at an acceptable level. Promotion from grade to grade and graduation from high school is dependent upon passing a test presumably based on them, a consequence that has triggered much debate about the benefits and liabilities of such promotions policies, particularly in large cities, such as Chicago and New York. Critics allege misreporting of test results and significant increases in the dropout rate in many cities, including Houston, Texas, where George W. Bush's first secretary of education, Rod Paige, was formerly superintendent. Thus far, all states but Iowa, a state that has traditionally led national indicators of academic achievement, have established such standards.

Tremendous angst has been expended over these state standards, which vary enormously. Mostly they have been defined as "what students know and are able to do" but they have been measured by tests, an important but limited mode of performance. Like the standards, the tests vary a great deal from state to state, most being decidedly less demanding than the NAEP. A few states, mostly ones in New England, have more highly regarded standards and tests that give results similar to NAEP. In some instances questions on the tests were being retrofitted into "standards" so that "teaching to the test" became the same as teaching the standards, a circularity that dramatically reduced the scope of the curriculum. Gradually the tests, which are much more limited than the standards generally, have become the focus. If the item is not on the test, it is

Characteristic student activity in 2004, triggered by the No Child Left Behind legislation, involved taking tests; these are students in Durham, North Carolina. *Courtesy of Kestrel Heights School*

unlikely to be taught. Mostly, however, what has been lost is what is not being tested, particularly the arts.

These standards began as a means of compelling schools, particularly ones with significant numbers of low-achieving students, to improve the quality of instruction provided to these pupils and hence to increase their learning. Shanker, for example, believed this was an effective strategy, but Howe did not, fearing that these children would not have an "opportunity to learn" the subject matter and would be penalized as a result. In the roiling politics of the turn of the century opportunity-to-learn issues vanished from most public debate, and were replaced with discussions of the adequacy of the tests used to demonstrate mastery of the standards.

During the 1980s and 1990s, however, before the enthusiasm for testing had reached its current heights, scholars in most academic fields gathered their wish lists for what students should be taught about their fields. Unlike the curriculum reforms of the 1960s, these efforts were intended for all students, not just college-bound ones, and most groups preparing these standards were not limited to the "best minds" but included individuals with experience in schools.

Mathematics reform was the first and the most deviant from what was being taught in schools. Math as a field had undergone reforms in the 1960s under the banner of "new math," but these reforms had apparently not penetrated into the belly of school arithmetic. Number facts and multiplication tables were still taught, but in 1989 the National Council of Teachers of Mathematics proposed standards focusing on concepts and problem-solving as well as computation. However, as scholar David K. Cohen explained in his 1990 article "A Revolution in One Classroom: The Case of Mrs. Oublier," which became a bible of the reform movement, even a California teacher, Mrs. O., with the best will in the world, who believed herself to be well prepared through her professional development experiences, was unable to understand this new—to her—mathematics and, therefore, unable to explain it to her students. Cohen wrote, "She [was] a thoughtful and committed teacher, but working as she did near the surface of this subject, many elements of understanding and many pedagogical possibilities remained invisible. Mathematically she was on thin ice. Because she did not know it, she skated smoothly on with great confidence."

History standards faced a different kind of attack: first, they were too extensive. As the renowned Yale historian Edmund Morgan allegedly remarked, he would be pleased if his doctoral students in history had such a command of their subject. Second, standards embraced too broadly the past of the poor and did not place enough emphasis on the past of leaders. John Adams did not get as much attention in the texts as George Washington Carver, and Harriet Beecher Stowe was discussed but not John F. Kennedy, critics charged. On the whole the new standards included much more material than could be taught in the present academic calendar by the current teaching force in American schools. Few suggestions on what could legitimately be cut were given, and teachers inevitably dropped what they could not handle.

NO CHILD LEFT BEHIND

As the standards movement accelerated after the turn of the century, the focus became the tests themselves. The focus on testing and the penalties for failing the tests intensified with Congress's passage in 2002 of the No Child Left Behind legislation (an incongruous title for a law that did, in fact, leave many children behind). Advanced by the Bush administration, this reauthorization of the 1965 ESEA, which like ESEA has an honorable goal, is encountering as much or more difficulty in implementation as did the original legislation.

One focus of the controversy is the law's mandate of frequent testing of pupils to determine the schools' adequacy and the children's knowledge. If the pupils fail, they now are likely to repeat the grade. If enough pupils in the school fail, the school itself is subject to various sanctions, including greater oversight of its activities by the authorities and public acknowledgment of its failure.

Teaching to the test has become the issue of the day. If the tests were themselves insightful and comprehensive, such a strategy might be acceptable. But most tests are not suitable replacements for a lively and intellectually vigorous curriculum that engages students' interests and imaginations and inspires them to further investigations. This should be a prime function of schooling, and testing is unlikely to provide that inspiration.

Now students are given many more tests, many of which are machine-scored, which limits the kinds of responses that can be expected of the students. Most thoughtful observers recognize that some testing is important, but that testing by itself is an inadequate strategy for attaining universal academic achievement. Some other ideas are necessary.

IMPROVING TEACHERS AND TEACHING

Improving the academic quality of teaching and of teachers themselves became a central new idea during the achievement period. In earlier eras, teachers have been critiqued for various failings. According to critics, the teachers of the assimilation era were too often rigid. The teachers of the adjustment era may have loved the children, but they let them do whatever they wanted, providing inadequate discipline. During the access era, some teachers worked with the "gifted and talented," meanwhile white teachers were accused of racism, black teachers of incompetence, and nearly all teachers of being unable to manage a classroom that included children with disabilities, and all were supposed to correct these deficits with "sensitivity training." Of course, such charges were not fair to many teachers who defied these negative stereotypes. Teachers, on the other hand, have regularly and increasingly complained about the conditions of their work—the lack of respect they encounter, the increasing bureaucratization of their tasks, and their work schedule, faced with no office, phone, or other amenities associated with white-collar work. They have also expressed their resentment of the low and relentlessly arbitrary salary schedules for what most believe to be an important, difficult, and intellectually demanding job.

Academic achievement for all was a brand new challenge for teachers that went to the core of their work. They had never been expected in the past to accomplish this goal with all students, and sometimes there had been little pressure to do it with any. Fortunately, some children virtually taught themselves. No one knew how to transform an aging cohort (in the 1990s the median age of U.S. teachers was forty-two; 35 percent had ten to twenty years in the classroom, and 30 percent more than twenty years) into an intellectually and professionally agile teaching force. "Professional development," covering a wide variety of activities of decidedly mixed quality, became a popular activity for experienced teachers. All these workshops, classes, weekend meetings, and even summer institutes attempted to make teachers better at what they do, but until recently they were too often a hodgepodge of unfocused activities provided at considerable cost to the school system. And, none of these development activities was equivalent to providing a teacher with a stimulating and demanding liberal arts education with additional work in how to engage children in such learning.

The most common problem for American teachers was not that they were mean or stupid (for most were not), but that they had not had good educations themselves. The majority of American teachers attended nonselective colleges, and most did not take the most demanding courses in them. Without a rigorous education, the palliatives produced by professional development were of limited benefit. With considerable funds available to spend on this effort and despite many new companies who offered such programs, little consensus emerged on what actually needed to be done to "fix" the teachers, although Boston and other cities now require "coaching" and subject matter courses, particularly in mathematics, for teachers.

Attention turned to the training of new teachers, a preventive rather than remedial approach. Beginning the same year that *A Nation at Risk* was published, the Holmes Group, composed of faculty members from research universities with significant teacher preparation programs, came together to tackle the issue of improving teacher education. Its indefatigable leader, Judith Lanier, then dean of the School of Education at Michigan State University, had a vision of professionalization that she believed would improve the quality of the American school-teaching force and hence the learning of students. It involved a strong liberal arts undergraduate education followed by post-baccalaureate study at a school of education and placement in a professional development school (a school that demonstrated excellent teaching and learning).

Despite its many reports, some of which were insightful and challenging, the group dissipated. Lanier was absolutely correct to recognize inadequacies in the preparation of many teachers and the unwillingness of universities to devote adequate resources to this effort. Yet the prescriptions the group advocated have not yet come to pass. The political forces within universities did not coalesce to make the necessary changes. The sectors of higher education that train most teachers (largely precariously funded public institutions and some small private ones) often refer to their teacher training programs as their "cash cows" as with relatively limited investments large numbers of individuals are graduated with degrees and teaching credentials. Most administrations of such institutions were not eager to jeopardize that moneymaker. Academically selective colleges and universities generally have either no teacher education programs or very small ones, and most professors there are not likely to encourage their best students to enter public school teaching. Furthermore, no consensus developed among teacher educators and others interested in professional education that the Holmes proposals represented "the one best way" to prepare teachers.

Instead of the Holmes solution, competing groups have emerged to attract and sometimes to accredit new teachers. Teach for America, founded in 1989 by Wendy Kopp, then a Princeton undergraduate, has brought recent undergraduates principally from demanding liberal arts programs into difficult schools with some summer preparation and further support during the first teaching years. The strength of this effort is the quality of the individuals brought into teaching, an important fraction of whom choose education as their life's work after additional graduate study. Other alternatives to the classic teacher certification programs have developed throughout the nation. Their hallmark typically is enthusiastic and often, but not always, academically strong individuals of varied ages and backgrounds who eschew traditional teacher education programs but who want to work with students, frequently in difficult schools. Most have limited expertise in pedagogy; some develop it on the job, and some do not.

The largest effort has come from a collaboration of a leading teacher educator, Linda Darling-Hammond, now at Stanford University's School of Education, with the National Council for the Accreditation of Teacher Education (NCATE), headed by Arthur Wise, formerly her colleague at the Rand Corporation. Together they have led an effort to link the state process of teacher certification or licensing to the NCATE approval of the college or university teacher education programs. Previously one could be certified by a state to teach either by successfully completing a state-approved teacher education program at a college or university or by the state's individual review of one's transcript to see if the proper allocation of courses had been completed. Concerned about the low standards prevalent in many teacher education programs, NCATE and certification authorities in several states reached the political agreement that only graduates of NCATE-approved programs can be licensed to teach in those states, thereby putting pressure on reluctant institutions to get NCATE approval. The assumption has been that institutions meeting NCATE standards would produce better teachers than those meeting state requirements. Yet weak institutions typically get NCATE approval while many of the strongest universities have been unwilling to commit the resources or to agree to what they perceive as NCATE's excessively bureaucratic regulations.

Meanwhile, the problem of teacher inadequacy was highlighted in Massachusetts when in 1998 60 percent of aspiring teachers failed the new Massachusetts Teachers Test. After lowering the passing grade, 44 percent failed the test several months later. None of the questions dealt with pedagogy but rather with literacy and subject matter knowledge. Whatever the psychometric merits or deficiencies of the test, the results

2. Which of the following situations represents $2 \frac{2}{5} \div \frac{1}{4}$?

   A. A $2 \frac{2}{5}$-acre lot needs to be plowed. If four workers split the plowing evenly, how many acres will each person plow?

   B. One side of a one-fourth-square-foot rectangle is $2 \frac{2}{5}$ feet. How long is the other side?

   C. Alix sawed off one fourth of a $2 \frac{2}{5}$-yard log. How many yards did Alix saw off?

   D. Terry picked $2 \frac{2}{5}$ pounds of berries and put them into one-quarter-pound containers. How many containers of berries did Terry fill?

A sample question from the Massachusetts exam for middle-school math teachers. The correct answer is D. More than 41 percent of potential teachers failed the test in November 2004. *From the Massachusetts Department of Education website: http://www.mtel.nesinc.com/PDFs/MTEL_fld47TIB.pdf*

were devastating both to the hopeful teachers and to the institutions allegedly educating them. Of course, some institutions (such as MIT, Wellesley, and Harvard) had much higher fractions passing the tests; though they were not NCATE accredited, they had much more academically rigorous requirements for entrance than most schools meeting the NCATE requirements. The question to ask of colleges and universities was not how the school of education courses had failed their students, because this was not tested, but rather why these individuals had been admitted either to the college or the teacher education program at all given their academic deficiencies.

SCHOOLS OF EDUCATION'S CONTRIBUTION

Why, one might inquire, have schools of education been so slow to respond to the changing demands of the public for school performance? First, faculties at major research universities who were appointed at a time when they were to be judged on whether their research met the standards of the disciplines have not changed their priorities instantly. Neither have scholars whose primary interest is education policy, not practice. Furthermore, because of the shortage of research funding for education, new scholars have not found it easy to develop lines of inquiry that will assist primary and, especially, secondary schools in meeting their new obligation to ensure that all students learn academic material well.

Most major universities have some faculty who are, in fact, attentive to these issues, mostly but not exclusively in their schools of education. Anthony Bryk, now a professor of education and business at Stanford University, has labored to understand and to strengthen schools serving low-income children, using Chicago's public schools as his locus of improvement. Former Rand Corporation alumni, including Paul Hill at the University of Washington, Milbrey McLaughlin at Stanford, and Jeannie Oakes at UCLA, are all attending to educational needs of low-income children. Richard Murnane, a distinguished economist at the Harvard Graduate School of Education, has spent the last several years working in and with the Boston public schools to improve their effectiveness. Several former policy gurus, David K. Cohen at Michigan and Richard Elmore at Harvard, for example, have turned their attention to issues of educational practice. Unlike most educational researchers, these academics have received substantial funding, primarily from foundations and other nongovernmental sources. Together the work of these scholars simply exemplifies the broader efforts of their many other colleagues who now regard not just investigating but rather improving the academic achievement of public school youngsters, particularly ones from families of poverty, as a major priority. Both educational practice, as opposed to research and policy, and particularly the effects of poverty on academic achievement are relatively new interests for distinguished professors of education, alas.

The recent and profound shift in professorial interests in education has occurred in response to the current concerns about academic inadequacy of the young. Yet it is not easy. University administrators consistently believe that their schools of education house individuals who are not as competent to consider these matters as the faculty at their business, public policy, or other schools. One explanation for the growth of private foundations and think tanks devoted to educational policies is that they are to some degree exempt from the standards of the university. Sometimes that means they are more likely to follow an ideological line they find congenial, though university faculty members are by no means exempt from the influence of ideology. But the intellectual energy and professional vision to explore and develop new ways of informing and improving practice are in short supply everywhere. Conceptualizing the problems of practice has been a slow process. Without this understanding, efforts at improving practice are often fitful.

EDUCATIONAL RESEARCH AND ITS CHALLENGES

One ongoing dilemma has bedeviled researchers since their first investigations into education at the dawn of the twentieth century: research designs do not fit the lumpy realities of educational practice. Undoubtedly that is one of the reasons that evaluations of the voucher or choice plans have been equivocal. We have not known how to gauge if a child was benefiting from a voucher program other than by his or her test score. We have not been able with our current methodology to determine which features of the new school are enhancing the student's experience and which ones are retarding it and why such is the case.

While we know it is possible to create schools in which all or nearly all children prosper, we are not sure exactly what the constituent ingredients of such schools are. We know that they can exist for we have seen them, but we do not know how to construct or universalize them. We know, for example, that there needs to be "alignment" between what the schools believe is necessary for the student to learn and what the families and communities (both the neighborhood and the nation) want for their youngsters. For most Americans today that means, as Anthony Bryk urges, a "rich intellectual environment with a challenging academic curriculum." We know that there must be substantial supports to enable the child to master the curriculum. We know that the children's fundamental health needs, both physical and mental, must be met. We know that respect must pervade the school: respect for the children, for their families, for the local and broader community, for the teachers, for the administrative staff, and for the educational endeavor in which they are all engaged. We also know that the teachers must have the skills themselves to teach the material and to assist the children in learning it, and the environment must be conducive to these activities. We also know that the leadership of the principal in support of these activities is vital.

Even if we are able to name the categories, we have not yet become able to organize the practices that follow from these categories. Many schools while professing allegiance to such principles simply do not embrace them in their daily life. Our evaluation methodologies are much better at documenting policies that have been established than they are at discerning those practices which interact together to create conditions for a good school. As the evaluation expert Carol Weiss has observed, we lack a strong social theory of schooling, and lacking the theory the evaluator has little against which to measure the existing practice.

Perhaps another way to express our schooling dilemma is that we treat schools as doughnuts. We are very good at explaining the periphery (the demographics of the students, the teachers, the funding), but we do not understand the hole in the center (what makes the child learn). The center is the essence of schooling, where the fundamental, but frequently unstated, priorities of education are generated, and our explicit understanding of that is a void. All the rest—student test scores, teacher pay, length of school term, attendance of students and teachers—are simply indicators on the periphery, mere proxies for the essence of the educational enterprise.

Deeply understanding the culture, the constraints, and the opportunities of schooling was not high on the intellectual agenda of educational researchers for much of the twentieth century, although by the end of the century some important work was beginning to be done on these issues. At least one explanation for this oversight was the lack of money for the task. Money for educational research has always been scarce in comparison with what we spend for other worthwhile activities, such as research on health, agriculture, or defense. Much of the funding for researching education during the last several decades has come from foundations and universities and gone to well-defined, specific activities, not to speculative theory-building work. Funders have been drawn to "implementation research," which means investigating the effects of new projects being adopted by schools. However, sometimes several new projects are begun simultaneously, and the combination dramatically complicates understanding the effects of one as opposed to another or the interactions among them.

In a nation that has traditionally believed in research and development in other fields, there has been precious little "R" on which to base the "D" in education. During the Reagan, Bush, and Clinton years the federal government, the primary funder of educational research, reduced its expenditures for this activity by 82 percent, according to a National Academy of Sciences study led by Richard Atkinson, former head of the National Science Foundation and later president of the University of California. Diane Ravitch, former assistant secretary of education, placed the drop at 90 percent from 1975 to 1995. For example, in 1989 the federal government's poorly funded educational research agency, OERI, spent less than $2 million (5 percent of its budget) on basic research in education while the Agriculture Research Service spent 46.6 percent; the National Institute of Health, nearly 60 percent; and the National Science Foundation, 93.5 percent, and all their budgets were much, much larger than OERI's. Various parts of the government, both inside the withered Department of Education and outside it, have continued to spend on specific research projects, but no wholesale effort to attack the problem of greater academic achievement through deeper understanding has occurred. There has been no comparable effort of NASA's "man on the moon" initiative of the 1960s in education.

In the changing culture of the academy of the last half of the twentieth century a good deal of "educational research" has been conducted, much of it on a financial shoestring and without significant quality control. Specialized journals have multiplied, many of them "peer-reviewed," but if one writes for a few like-minded associates, such peer review does not assure high quality. Similarly, the organization of educational researchers, the American Educational Research Association, despite varied efforts to improve its programs, has not yet managed to exemplify excellence.

Research continues on "standards": how do you develop them and how do you implement them? These are worthy topics and should be supported with research dollars. But neither gets to the fundamental question of achievement for all: what are the school, home, and community conditions that are essential for maximum academic achievement, defined as capacity to function smoothly in a rich intellectual environment, and how do we ensure that we have them?

We also need to know what regulatory restrictions and freedoms are necessary for schools to flourish. Are unions an impediment to achieving academic success, and if so, how and if not, why not? How important is money absolutely, and how important is flexibility in use of discrete income flows? In good schools, defined as above, does mixing racial, ethnic, and social class of students, faculty, or administrative staff make a difference, and if so, what differences and why? How does one assure that mastery of academic material includes support not only for "the right answer" but also for ingenuity, imagination, and ultimately fascination with some subjects? Ultimately, is academic achievement alone a sufficient goal for American schools serving our democracy or do we need also to attend to imagination, honesty, teamwork, civic participation, and fair play?

FIVE

Autonomy to Accountability

WHEN IS SCHOOLING COMPLETE? At the beginning of the twentieth century most Americans believed they had "completed" their schooling if they finished the eighth grade. Only 6 percent of young people then graduated from high school. Eighth-grade graduation was a major celebration, particularly in rural neighborhoods, with the newly recognized scholars feted and dressed in their best as the photograph of my father's 1908 Ottertail County, Minnesota, eighth-grade class illustrates. In 1955 a ninth-grade student in my homeroom, when queried how far her father had gone in school, replied confidently, "all the way." That meant high school graduation in the Deep Creek, Virginia, neighborhood. By the end of the twentieth century, however, that definition had changed radically. "Completing schooling" now means some college at a minimum, with about 66 percent of high school graduates now attending, and increasingly it has meant acquiring a post-graduate degree.

These changing expectations for what is considered sufficient schooling have dramatically altered American views of higher education. Once thought the domain of the very few (less than 2 percent of the age group in 1900) and largely peripheral to the economy, colleges and universities occupied a very different position at the beginning of the twenty-first century. They now appeal to a mass population, and they constitute a crucial link in the economy through their research and development activities. Furthermore, unlike 1900 when few foreigners would ever have considered coming to the United States to study, they now attract both students and faculty from all over the world, including some of the most gifted and ambitious. The range of these institutions from the leading research universities, which remain among the best in the world, to "open enrollment" institutions (with no requirements for admission other than paying the tuition), which provide unparalleled access to higher education, is extraordinary. Today the academic overlap between some of the best high schools and some undergraduate institutions is considerable, with high school juniors and seniors flourishing in college classes.

FROM ISOLATED AND AUTONOMOUS TO INVOLVED AND ACCOUNTABLE

At the beginning of the twentieth century, American colleges were isolated, impoverished, and intellectually weak. Most were located in rural areas and small towns, the product of their religious origins in which competitive denominations had founded colleges, inevitably small, and culturally homogeneous. Faculties were small and largely unspecialized with the president typically teaching the capstone course, moral philosophy. Students ranged in age from early teens, typically enrolled in the "preparatory department" intended as an alternative to high school, to early twenties. Attending a term or two was much more common than acquiring a degree, which had limited utility.

In fact, higher education enrollments in the United States had declined during the latter years of the nineteenth century as most young people chose a different destiny than college. Obligations of citizenship certainly did not require it; many presidents of the United States, even as late as Warren G. Harding (1920–1924), were not college graduates. Many highly intelligent persons who sought a career in business did not think college vital for success. Many lawyers, doctors, and ministers did not obtain full college diplomas before entering their professional studies. Elementary teachers (the vast majority of teachers in the early twentieth century) simply needed to finish eighth grade and have a term or two of normal school. Of course, some sought college degrees simply because they (or their parents for them) wanted a convivial setting in which to learn more. Yet if citizenship did not require higher education and jobs did not, few in the early twentieth century chose to spend either the time or the money on it.

Even the Ivy League institutions, most founded before the Revolution, were a little sleepy, although Charles William Eliot, president of Harvard from 1869 to 1909, successfully led a broadening of the college's curriculum from a common set of courses for all to one that included electives and hence required the faculty to specialize. In 1904, Princeton's undergraduate enrollment was 665, making it sixteenth in total enrollments in the United States. Its president, Woodrow Wilson, directed the new, and bitterly fought for, graduate school, which again broke free from the limited curriculum of classics, philosophy, ancient history, and a modicum of science and mathematics, and required professors to become specialists in academic disciplines. Nonetheless, Wilson observed of new faculty, "If their qualities as gentlemen and scholars conflict, the former will win them the place."

Essentially, the public paid little attention to higher education during the first half of the twentieth century, primarily because so few Americans participated in it and because it appeared to contribute so little of importance to the society. Americans who worried about the future of their country before 1950 and about the role of educational institutions in it concentrated on the schools, not the colleges. Only within the last sixty years have colleges and universities come to be seen as vitally important for national development, both in terms of the kinds of opportunities they provide for students and in terms of the research and outreach they devote to solving societal problems.

During the first half of the twentieth century, American higher education functioned relatively autonomously, setting its course and reaching its destination with modest involvement from outside forces. Because colleges and universities were not perceived to be very important to the society, they were essentially independent. If they were able to find enough tuition-paying students and, for the public institutions, convince enough state legislators (some of whom they hoped were their satisfied alumni) to support their funding requests, then they were reasonably secure. Endowments were modest, and most survived on annual budgets of tuition and appropriations.

The second half of the twentieth century, however, brought dramatic changes in the perceived significance to the society of colleges and universities and, consequently, remarkable increases in funding, largely from outside sources, many of them governmental. Two principal issues explain the shift. First, the nation recognized the vital contribution of research both to national defense and to the national economy and was convinced that universities were the best place to undertake it.

Second, there was a growing understanding that more students than previously believed could benefit from higher education and that the economy needed better trained workers.

As a consequence of their increasing centrality to America, higher education institutions became much more subject to influence, and scrutiny, from the outside world. By the end of the twentieth century, college was as common for Americans as high school had been in the 1960s. Furthermore, the research conducted on American campuses now leads the world, a situation that could not have been conceived in 1900. Concentrations of able, diverse, lively, committed young people have populated American campuses since the 1960s and have triggered or escalated many of the social issues of the last fifty years. Each of these changes made the institutions less autonomous and more accountable.

INFANT INSTITUTIONS IN 1900

A century ago when Americans were proud of the public schools and their rapid growth, we had little comparable pride in our institutions of higher education. No American university matched the best of England or Europe for graduate work or probably even for undergraduate study. People with money who were interested in advanced scholarship routinely sought research opportunities at Oxford, Cambridge, or one of the established universities on the Continent or at the Kaiser Wilhelm Institutes in Germany. Paris, Berlin, London, and Zurich were all places of high culture and esteemed learning, and even more distant places such as Warsaw, Copenhagen, Stockholm, and Prague had cosmopolitan and erudite circles. New York City and Chicago, let alone Washington, D.C., did not have such standing. Today, however, our finest universities, even those in "college towns"—such as Berkeley and Palo Alto, California; Madison, Wisconsin; Ann Arbor, Michigan; or Cambridge, Massachusetts—attract both students and faculty from all over the world and are regarded by their international peers as among the best in the world. Even our institutions of considerably less academic stature, of which there are many, draw international students who deem them preferable to what would be available to them at home.

Prior to World War II American colleges and universities differed from each other primarily by curriculum and by clientele. Throughout the first half of the twentieth century it was relatively easy to identify what was taught and what was expected of graduates of various types of institutions. The dominant institution was the liberal arts college, whose curriculum embodied the traditional academic disciplines of the humanities—Greek; Latin; philosophy; religion; European literature; history of the ancient world, Europe, and the United States; mathematics; a smattering of the emerging social sciences (economics, sociology, political science, and anthropology); and a little science. State universities, especially those supported by federal funds from the Morrill Acts of 1862 and 1890 and the Hatch Act of 1887, haltingly established research and teaching programs in engineering, agriculture, and home economics as required by the legislation. Not until the 1890s, thirty years after the passage of the first Morrill Act, however, with the introduction of the Babcock test for milk fat devised at the University of Wisconsin, did any of the institutions have a useful, commercially viable product from their efforts. No wonder farmers were reluctant to send their children to study at these places.

The research university was in its infancy in the early twentieth century. Institutions such as Amherst and Yale were quite similar places in 1890 but very different in 1950, the former having remained a liberal arts college and the latter having transformed itself into a university. The state universities, some of which became leaders in research, were gaining prominence for their incorporation of the classical studies found in the liberal arts institutions with the practical work in engineering, agriculture, and home economics. In the 1920s, teachers colleges, nearly all of which became state universities, emerged gradually from precollegiate normal schools into four-year institutions awarding the bachelor's degree, initially providing a mix of liberal arts curriculum and pedagogical studies for individuals intending to teach in public schools.

The institutions best identified by the homogeneity of their clientele, historically black colleges, women's colleges, and Roman Catholic colleges, provided a distinctive environment for their students. Many of the most prestigious liberal arts colleges were for men only, primarily white Protestant men (Harvard, Yale, Columbia, Princeton, Dartmouth, Brown, Amherst, Williams, Bowdoin, Haverford, with only Wabash remaining today as male only).

FRANKLIN COLLEGE AS A MODAL INSTITUTION CIRCA 1900

By far the most numerous institutions were the small, impecunious, and denominationally affiliated liberal arts colleges sprinkled across the American landscape. One such institution, Franklin College in Franklin, Indiana, where my grandfather Columbus Horatio Hall was professor of Greek and Latin and vice president from the late nineteenth century until World War I, typified the Baptist version of the genre. With early-twentieth-century enrollments of less than two hundred, most of whom were in the preparatory department (today what we would consider the equivalent of grades seven to twelve), the college faculty and administration numbered about a dozen. Always short of funds, such colleges served a local and homogeneously Protestant constituency including boys and girls, and sent a few of their graduates to distinguished careers in higher education and public service while most remained in the region as well-educated members of their communities.

Faculty at Franklin generally did not have advanced degrees other than occasional divinity degrees, which Hall had acquired when he became a Baptist minister. Only the professor of Latin then had a Ph.D. Their primary function was teaching, not research, although Hall occasionally noted in his diary his ongoing study of Greek prepositions during his two months of summer camping on an island in Lake Superior. He left no record of any publications about the prepositions. More often, however, he commented on his reading, particularly of Ralph Waldo Emerson about whom he observed, "He is fresh in his statements of facts and theories but always wrong in his central principle of philosophy." He did prepare one article, "Christianity and Culture," for the college quarterly. Hall apparently did not aspire to be a scholar; rather, he sought the nonspecialized life of an academic combined with administrative responsibility, teaching, and ministry. He wished his summer to be spent in rest, reading, and reflection, with some minimal attention to the Greek prepositions. His students were similar to my mother, Marguerite, and her eight brothers and sisters: white, middle class, Baptist in family origin. Most came from within a one-hundred-mile radius of Franklin. The nearest city was the state capital, Indianapolis, which was twenty miles away by interurban trolley, and provided the nearest cultural opportunities.

STATE UNIVERSITIES EMERGE

My father, Victor Lincoln Albjerg, on the other hand, illustrates the changing emphases within higher education. His college teaching career began in 1927 (just after Hall's ended) but almost twenty years after he had begun teaching in a one-room rural school in Minnesota. He never studied Latin, then still considered the mark of an "educated man." He had attended a liberal arts college (Hamline in St. Paul, Minnesota) only briefly. Rather, he came to believe as World War I began and he became less provincial in his outlook that better and cheaper education was available at the state university. He graduated from the University of Minnesota, which no longer required Latin, though it did require one foreign language (Spanish, French, German, Latin, or Greek). Upon graduation he entered the U.S. Navy as an ensign and served in the Atlantic and Europe.

Ultimately Victor believed that he needed graduate work in an academic discipline if he was going to teach at the college level, and he received a Ph.D. in history from the University of Wisconsin. At Wisconsin in a doctoral seminar in American history he noticed an attractive, articulate fellow student, the only woman in the class. She was Marguerite Hall, who had entered graduate school after the death of her fiancé in World War I. Her brother, Arnold, a professor of political science at Wisconsin, urged her to get a Ph.D. since as a single woman she would need to support herself. Marguerite had expected to remain single, but she was drawn to Victor, both for his skills as a historian and for his breadth of talents, including ski jumping off Bascom Hill, a steep slope in the center of the Madison campus. Victor believed that he should be able to support her before they married. He accepted a position at Purdue, where he taught for

At the beginning of the twentieth century the Purdue University campus in West Lafayette, Indiana, revealed a few scattered buildings, including a mechanics' shop, a laboratory house, an industrial arts hall, a military hall, an engine house, and University Hall (for everything else). The bleak landscape characterized the land-grant university with no endowment in 1900. *Courtesy of Special Collections, Purdue University Library*

thirty-six years. When he arrived in 1927, he was one of two history professors with a Ph.D., the remaining history faculty having bachelor's or master's degrees only. He also understood that his main emphasis was teaching: four courses each semester and two each summer. No two months of summer camping on Lake Superior for him! His professorial salary was such that he and Marguerite could only afford a rented upstairs apartment in a local house until they spent their savings intended for his European sabbatical year (can-

celed in 1940, due to World War II) to build a new house. Despite that heavy schedule, he also did research, culminating in four books and many articles.

Purdue was one of the Morrill Act institutions, created to serve the needs of the state and its citizens. On the West Lafayette campus, those needs were not perceived to include studies in history, which was referred to as a "service department," providing ancillary studies for the important "majors." Rather, the heart of the institution was its engineering school, supported by strong science departments, followed by its well-regarded agriculture school and its agricultural extension outreach program. The liberal arts subjects existed as peripheral studies, and through the 1950s the only baccalaureate degree available was a bachelor of science (the degree I hold with an undergraduate major in English). Thus, the state universities created through the Morrill Act primarily served the economic interests of the state, with a very different hierarchy of prestigious subjects than at the liberal arts colleges. As a student at Purdue one "washed out" from high status chemical engineering to low status political science or history. In the Ivy League, on the other hand, liberal arts studies were high status subjects and engineering slightly déclassé.

When Victor began teaching at Purdue, enrollment was slightly more than three thousand, but by the time he retired in 1963 it was just under eighteen thousand, making it one of the country's larger, but by no means largest, universities. Fellow students at Purdue were likely to be Hoosier compatriots except in the nationally recognized engineering fields, where even New Yorkers attended, as did neighbors from Ohio, Illinois, Michigan, and Kentucky. Despite the university's growth and increasing complexity, my father remained committed to his students as individuals. As part of his teaching, each semester my father invited the students in his classes to attend a tea at our house where my mother presided using her inherited silver tea service. He saw instruction in history as only part of the socialization these students deserved to receive from college, particularly for those students like him who came from rural, immigrant, or economically circumscribed backgrounds.

The Purdue students were a little more heterogeneous than the ones at Franklin as Roman Catholics and Jews were added to the predominantly Protestant mix, though both Catholics and Jews had their own separate fraternities. Catholics were accepted into the national fraternities and sororities, which provided a vital social network on the campus, but practicing Jews were not. Blacks were also prohibited from the Greek system. A few students from outside the United States attended, most noticeable when they ate alone at the student union cafeteria during the holidays.

As the late and renowned judge Leon Higginbotham revealed in the introduction to his *In the Matter of Race*, black students were not welcomed at Purdue. They were prohibited from living in university student housing when he entered in 1944. Later Higginbotham attributed his decision to shift from engineering to law to the president of Purdue's statement to him, "Higginbotham, the law doesn't require us to let colored students in the dorm, we will never do it, and you either accept things as they are or leave the university immediately." Higginbotham left and graduated from Yale Law School seven years later. Black adults were not welcome as residents of West Lafayette, nor were Jews in most neighborhoods, until well after World War II. When black students enrolled at Purdue in large numbers as a result of the GI Bill, the barbershop at the student union building refused to cut their hair, prompting my father to boycott his longtime barber and travel to Mulberry, Indiana, for a trim.

When Purdue hired one of its first Jewish professors, the distinguished Viennese physicist Karl Lark-Horowitz, he and his wife found housing across the Wabash River in Lafayette. Lark-Horowitz exemplified the best in modern physics, both in his own work and in the colleagues he selected to bring to Purdue either as regular faculty or visiting lecturers. Yet at the Purdue of his era (1928–1958), the transition to a research university was not yet complete. The institution was not fully committed to research itself or to supporting the finest scholars regardless of their religion, ethnicity, or gender. As the Purdue physics department's history, recounted in its 2003 website, reveals,

> Although many first-rate physicists [e.g., Hans Bethe, Robert Oppenheimer, Emilio Segre, Edward Teller, Werner

Heisenberg, I. I. Rabi, Arthur Compton, E. O. Lawrence] visited the university for various lengths of time during this period [1935–42], few remained. The University was still recovering from the Depression, but there was another factor at work. Some of these visitors were Jewish refugees who had been driven from Germany and Italy. . . . Unfortunately, most American universities did not welcome Jewish refugees as warmly as one might hope, and Purdue was apparently little different.

An American Jew was denied a permanent position, the report continued, "due to anti-Semitism among the higher administrative officials." At the time the much-beloved dean of the school of engineering and subsequently acting president of Purdue, A. A. Potter, a regular attendee of Central Presbyterian Church, was, in fact, a Russian Jew who had emigrated early in the century. At his death in 1979 the local rabbi conducted his service, much to the astonishment of many of his friends.

Purdue was reluctant to welcome any talented scholars who were not male, Christian, and white, as Marguerite Hall Albjerg soon discovered. She actually received her Ph.D. in history from Wisconsin and published her first scholarly article before Victor did. Her first position after receiving her degree was in the history department at Alabama State College for Women in Montevallo. She became chair of the department, a position she left to marry Victor after he began teaching at Purdue. Despite her persistent efforts and considerable research and publications, she was never able to secure a regular faculty appointment at Purdue from the time she arrived in 1928 until Victor's retirement in 1963. She was frequently called upon to lead "quiz sections" in large lecture courses taught by men with master's degrees and no research activity. She was highly regarded as a teacher but various explanations were given for her lack of regular appointment, one of which was the university rule outlawing nepotism that was enunciated during the depression. On the other hand, when many male faculty were engaged in World War II and Purdue was short-handed, she was hired to teach sociology, a subject she had never formally studied. When the shortage was over, she was dismissed despite excellent teaching reviews and some relevant publications. Pedagogical skill and scholarly productivity were not the prime determinants of faculty appointments at Purdue or most other universities of that era. Fitting into the collegial culture was more important, as Woodrow Wilson had attested earlier at Princeton.

One of Victor's duties as a history professor in the 1930s and 1940s was to chair the Purdue "convocations committee," which brought culture to the Hoosier cornfields. Unlike the musically gifted Lark-Horowitz, he had little musical sophistication, being partially deaf in one ear and tone deaf in both. Yet he brought to his task deep commitment and boundless energy to find the best musicians and other cultural figures and bring them to as many people as possible at Purdue. These popular events played to capacity audiences in the Hall of Music (nearly as large as Rockefeller Center, the proud Boilermakers, as the Purdue faithful are known, announced) and featured Eugene Ormandy with the Philadelphia Symphony Orchestra and other leading philharmonics, international ballet troupes, the Metropolitan Opera, and individual musicians, including violinist Zino Francescatti. Less highbrow entertainment, such as regular visits from Bob Hope, were included as well. These events attracted not only students, faculty, and local townspeople, but also Hoosiers from throughout the state who bought season "convo" tickets. Along with its support for classical music on the local radio station, WBAA, the Voice of Purdue, the university understood its role to serve the state not only through its instruction but through outreach in subject areas such as agriculture and home economics and in culture as well. Many of the stations making up the National Public Radio network today began as university radio stations in the years between the world wars.

Even during Victor's years on the faculty, athletics was important, filling the streets of West Lafayette on fall Saturday afternoons with cars bringing families to support the Boilermakers' efforts to subdue traditional football rivals Notre Dame and Indiana and to win in the Big Ten. In winter emphasis shifted to basketball, a sport my father preferred, as many of the team members sought degrees with high school social studies teaching credentials, necessitating enrolling in my father's history courses. One of them, a particularly gifted student and player, intended to teach high school history in Fort Wayne and coach basketball, but John Wooden ended up coaching at UCLA. During these years all the athletic activities were encompassed with a women's gymnasium (the former men's gym), a field house, and a stadium, modest but adequate facilities befitting a Big Ten university.

Victor reached age seventy and under mandatory retirement rules then in effect retired from Purdue in 1963, leaving a much larger (enrollment was six times greater) and more cosmopolitan institution than the one he had joined in 1927. Most of the changes came following World War II. One unfortunate interlude in the early 1950s included a brief but intense period of public questioning of the university and of him for teaching Russian history during the beginnings of the Cold War. This occurred in the state that was home to both the Ku Klux Klan and the John Birch Society. Tenure saved him. Purdue, like many universities whose faculties were attacked on these issues, protected their tenured faculty while letting their nontenured colleagues swing in the wind of public criticism.

Still wishing to teach and to participate professionally, Victor accepted a postretirement appointment at St. Norbert College in West DePere, Wisconsin, and here again he found himself at an institution in the midst of a monumental transition. Like most Catholic colleges in America, St. Norbert's was then shifting from being an institution run by Catholics, mostly members of religious orders, for Catholic youth to one in which clerics were in the minority in both faculty and administration and many students and faculty members were non-Catholic. The curriculum had a relatively narrow liberal arts focus with an important component of Roman Catholic theology and culture. The faculty, both cleric and lay, emphasized teaching, not research, and believed the necessary outcome for their graduates was that they be both educated and Catholic. New ideas were not as important as truths.

Victor, a deeply humane man, was not a believer and had rejected both the Lutheran and Danish Baptist traditions of his youth for what he termed a "congenial agnosticism." At St. Norbert's he was one of the first non-Catholics hired on the faculty and was asked to begin his teaching with a course on Renaissance and Reformation history, a ticklish subject in that environment. St. Norbert's, however, welcomed him warmly and while there he witnessed the departure of clerical administrators and faculty for secular lives, the broadening of the curriculum, and a diminishing Roman Catholic influence.

Just as Columbus Horatio Hall's work at Franklin College captures the dominant mode of higher education at the beginning of the century, so Victor's extensive experience at Purdue and his more limited tenure at St. Norbert's encapsulate much that occurred in American higher education in the middle years of the century. First, public institutions became the dominant ones in terms of enrollment, serving a minority of college students until 1950 but now nearly 80 percent. Second, the curriculum dramatically expanded from the limited classics cum math and a smidgen of science common to the small liberal arts colleges to the multidepartment, academic disciplines common to colleges and universities today. Purdue, for example, included all its social sciences in one department until after World War II when history, government, economics, and sociology (plus philosophy) split into separate units. Anthropology came later. Third, universities became more important to the nation than colleges had been in the first half of the twentieth century, thereby forcing faculty selection from primarily the criterion of collegiality to one of potentiality of research contribution. The role of teaching faded at most places in this shift. Finally, Roman Catholic institutions, the largest group of denominational colleges, underwent a profound change as local priests no longer insisted to faithful Catholics that only a Catholic institution would be appropriate for their children, as priests and nuns left their orders in large numbers, and as faculties became increasingly secular and often non-Catholic.

Marguerite's experience was also typical of women who sought academic careers, largely because she married and attempted to have a career similar to and in the same neighborhood as her husband. Women with Ph.D.s in the first two thirds of the twentieth century found it extremely difficult to get academic employment except in women's colleges (of which there were very few) or in very small, nonresearch institutions. A woman Ph.D. in Tippecanoe County, Indiana, therefore, had few options, as my mother discovered despite her ample qualifications. A metropolitan area would have given her more options, but probably not in research universities, which rarely hired women professors until the 1970s. Only one woman taught regularly in the social sciences at Purdue in my mother's time, a widow without a Ph.D.

NICHE COLLEGES

As Roman Catholic colleges lost their distinctiveness after World War II, so too did others that had previously served a particular niche. Normal schools intended to prepare public school teachers became state teachers colleges in the 1920s before changing their names and sometimes their curriculum to become state colleges and then state universities in the postwar years. Women's colleges, both public and private, increasingly became coeducational beginning in the late 1960s, coincident with previously all-male colleges admitting women.

Most blacks who sought an undergraduate degree in the first half of the century did so in chronically underfunded historically black colleges, partly because most blacks then lived in the South and were prohibited from attending a white institution. Today slightly less than 13 percent of black undergraduates attend historically black colleges and universities. Such institutions have stressed the positive benefits for their students, who do not have to face the often-hostile academic environment such as the one Leon Higginbotham encountered as a freshman at Purdue. In 1938 the Supreme Court gave its first indication that higher education's pattern of racial segregation would be challenged in *Gaines* v. *Canada*. The cases addressing segregation began with law schools, because judges, who had graduated from law schools, could recognize that the "equal" requirements of "separate but equal" were not being met when separate law schools were established for blacks.

A mattress-making course at the Tuskegee Normal and Industrial Institute passed as higher education for African American women in Alabama at the beginning of the twentieth century. *Library of Congress, Prints & Photographs Division, [LC-USZ62-24334]*

Thus, the first half of the twentieth century saw most higher education institutions serving distinct constituencies with specific curricula. By 1940, 9 percent of the young people were attending college (a number that increased significantly during the depression when jobs were scarce), with 8 percent graduating. National scholarships did not exist, so attendance was likely to be at a local college unless one came from a family of wealth that could afford a distant institution. The curriculum was tailored to either a general liberal arts program or a specific vocational specialty, such as teaching, engineering, home economics, or accounting. Because most institutions drew students from the local community, homogeneity characterized most places; heterogeneity was a little suspect. Teaching was the fundamental activity; research was rare. Research of high quality was even rarer. Activities intended to edify and to amuse both the student body and the larger community proliferated.

WORLD WAR II BRINGS PROFOUND CHANGES

What caused the profound transformation of these small and sleepy colleges to the immense and dynamic universities during the last century? The simplest answer is World War II. The Second World War, which the United States entered in 1941, two years after it began, and which ended in 1945, changed American higher education in three fundamental dimensions, each of which still characterizes it today. First, the war effort demanded solutions to critical problems that could be achieved only through research, and universities were the places in the United States where most researchers worked and learned how to investigate. The Manhattan Project, which resulted in the creation of the atomic bomb, consisted of professors working on their home campuses and ultimately in a consortium in New Mexico. Prior to World War II, while some professors had engaged in research, it had not been a mainstay of professorial activity. Today it is still not the principal professional activity of many professors, but at our best institutions research is universally expected of faculty whether it is undertaken or not.

Second, the passage of the GI Bill in 1944, more formally known as the Servicemen's Readjustment Act, which provided college scholarships for veterans among other benefits, profoundly altered the undergraduate student body. Like so many pieces of legislation, the unintended consequences of the GI Bill were much more important than its intended one, which was to keep returning veterans from moving too swiftly into job searches and thereby causing unemployment in an economy lurching from wartime to peacetime activities. The notion was that the vets could cool their heels in college while dribbling back into the peacetime workforce, rather than glutting the market with unemployed veterans seeking jobs.

The effect of the GI Bill on undergraduate life was astonishing as these adults, often married men with families, eschewed the traditional undergraduate fraternity pranks and concentrated on their studies in an effort to get their degrees, make up for lost time, and get on with their lives. University presidents, such as Chicago's Robert Maynard Hutchins and Harvard's James B. Conant, despaired at the prospect of these "unprepared" students descending upon them and weakening their selective student bodies. Hutchins observed that campuses would become "educational hobo jungles," evoking the unemployed men who had ridden the rails during the depression. Conant, having disparaged the vets originally, had the grace later to recognize that they had, in fact, turned out to be "the most mature and promising students Harvard has ever had." Many were the first in their families to attend college. What the vets did was demonstrate that a much higher fraction of the American public could achieve academically in college than had previously been believed. This realization opened the floodgate for much broader access to college for Americans and for federal financial aid to assist the needy and not-so-needy prospective students.

Third, as a result of Hitler's rise to power prior to World War II, many extremely gifted scholars, most of whom were Jewish, emigrated from Europe to the United States. Many sought employment as professors,

World War II veterans register at Harvard in September 1947. Despite Harvard University president Conant's initial concerns about veterans' intellectual abilities, these men raised the academic standards of the university as enrollment swelled from 1,826 in 1944 to more than 14,000 in September 1947. *Harvard University Archives Call # HUP-SF Student Life (56)*

the job they had held or had aspired to hold in their home countries. Faculties at leading American universities prior to 1940 were almost entirely white, male, and Christian. Many had never knowingly hired a Jewish professor, and most had either explicit or implicit quotas for admitting Jewish students. At midcentury it was not unusual for Jewish young men aspiring to the professoriat to change their names to something faintly English and sometimes their religious affiliation to Presbyterian or some other respected Protestant denomination. But the influx of outstanding Jewish scholars, particularly physicists and mathematicians whose skills were so essential in weapons research, jolted American higher education into recognizing such talents as Albert Einstein, Edward Teller, Stanislav Ulam, Hans Bethe, and Isidore I. Rabi. Jewish scholars, some émigrés and some native born, in other fields such as philosophy, art history, English, sociology, and history, joined leading university faculties in the 1940s and 1950s, thereby providing a cosmopolitanism that was new to the white-outfitted tennis players at Princeton. The overall effect was both to reinforce the broadening of college and university perspectives and to enhance the academic work at the institutions. Later, the leadership that American universities had shown in hiring and promoting Jews before leading banks, law firms, or major corporations did would slowly extend to racial minorities and to white women.

EMERGING DOMINANCE OF AMERICAN COLLEGES AND UNIVERSITIES

Higher education's past sixty years have been very different from the first four decades of the twentieth century. American colleges and universities have moved from the backwater to the mainstream of intellectual life, not just in the United States but in the world as well. Having been previously the province of the few, they have become the locale of the many. Isolation characterized many of the rural colleges of the nineteenth and early twentieth centuries, prompting many to decry their "ivory tower" separation. In the latter twentieth century, however, the majority of students populated institutions located in urban and suburban America. There they found themselves often in the forefront of social change and in the midst of the market economy. Today, critics have turned their attention to higher education, calling for "accountability" for the investments, financial and personal, that have been made in these institutions. The relative autonomy that characterized them for much of the nineteenth and early twentieth century, when they had to recruit paying students and satisfy mostly compliant state legislatures and, in some cases, religious institutions, seems long gone.

Just as the decade encompassing World War II brought a trio of changes, so also has the last half of the twentieth century brought three fundamental changes to American higher education: growth in the number of students and scope of activities, dominance of the research university ideal, and the emergence of schools as centers of social controversy and change. Each has engendered increased public attention to the institutions.

GROWTH

The emphasis on access in elementary and secondary education from 1954 to 1983 spread to higher education as well. As the economist Alice Rivlin has argued, the most significant of the initial rationales for passing the Higher Education Act of 1965, which provided financial aid for undergraduates, was social justice, providing opportunity for students from low-income families to get a college education. Of course, 1965 was also the year the Elementary and Secondary Education Act, also a mechanism for social justice for younger students, was passed. Two other reasons rapidly emerged and ultimately became determining in justifying federal support for the Higher Education Act: increasing economic growth and productivity of the workforce and providing for national security by getting or staying ahead of the Soviet Union technically and scientifically.

By any conceivable standard American higher education expanded enormously in the twentieth century, particularly the second half when not only the traditional age group (eighteen- to twenty-four-year-olds) increased their participation but also older Americans. During the twentieth century the number of undergraduates grew from 238,000 to more than 13,000,000. Participation in two-year community colleges, mostly in the second half of the century, accounts for more than 40 percent of the increase. From 1900 to 1940, growth was modest, from 2 to 9 percent of the age group enrolled. Thirty years later, however, 36 percent was enrolled, and by the end of the century about 55 percent of the traditional age group was enrolled. Currently about two-thirds of high school graduates enroll in college. Not all the enrollees receive bachelor's degrees, of course, particularly in recent years when many attend college just for a course or two. The pattern of attending college immediately after high school and graduating with a bachelor's degree in four or five years is now a minority pattern. Most who graduate take longer.

The United States still leads the world in college participation among twenty-five- to thirty-four-year-olds but has fallen behind in receipt of college degrees, where it now ranks second to Norway. For most of the last hundred years the United States has led substantially in percent of its youth who are college educated, although Canada, Japan, Belgium, and Greece are now closing the gap for some subsets of the population (males and youth). Today more than a third of American adults have attended post-secondary institutions, while comparable figures in other nations include about one-fifth of the Japanese and about one-tenth of those in western Europe. The principal explanation for the discrepancy is the higher fraction of Americans attending colleges in the earlier years of the twentieth century when other nations sent a significantly smaller fraction of their population to college.

Despite this increase in enrollments, students are still significantly stratified by family income and institution. In the nation's most selective colleges, many of which have large financial aid programs, 74 percent of the students come from the richest socioeconomic quartile and only 3 percent from the poorest. Department of Education researcher Clifford Adelman's studies of high school and college transcripts reveal that 70 percent of high school graduates from the wealthiest families earn bachelor's degrees, compared to 20 percent of those from the lowest-income families. These figures also testify, of course, to the better elementary and secondary schools serving the wealthy. Over the past twenty years loans have replaced grants as the predominant form of student aid for needy students, thus providing another hurdle for students from low-income families. Meanwhile, "merit based" grants have grown as semiselective colleges have sought to raise the average SAT scores of their student body by attracting and enrolling with scholarships high scorers regardless of their family's need for financial aid.

Faculties in the United States have grown as well, though proportionately not as much as undergraduates, from approximately 147,000 in 1940 to 729,000 in 1970 to a little more than 1,000,000 in 2000. Yet for many faculty, administrators, and new Ph.D.s the explanation of growth is misleading as it has occurred with many instances of retrenchment, especially affecting beginning faculty seeking teaching positions in the humanities and social sciences. These traditional liberal arts fields lost enrollments in the 1970s as general education requirements evaporated and preprofessional programs grew. Further, the increase in part-time faculty has reduced the opportunities for full-time faculty appointments in these fields, presumably preferable to many seeking a career in higher education. Generally institutions have made these decisions under pressure to cut costs, which have also risen regularly beyond the consumer price index. The explanation typically given for such increases is that most college costs are for personnel, which thus far have not proved amenable to comparable increases in their "productivity," which remains generally undefined. At prestigious universities, especially, the most highly paid faculty rarely have their teaching loads increased while part-time faculty are hired at lower salaries but often in large numbers to teach the growing student population.

With students and faculty growing, budgets have as well. The immediate years from World War II to the mid-1960s saw increases in federal support for research of nearly 25 percent annually. Overall from 1940 to 1994 organized research grew fifty-six times in constant (1994) dollars; instruction grew eighteen times; and administration grew thirty-seven times. From 1953 to 1963 alone federal money to universities increased 455 percent. One consequence of this remarkable increase in research funding was a concentration in a few institutions. By 1966, six universities received 57 percent of all federal research and development funds, and twenty institutions accounted for 79 percent of all the funds. These developments established a more rigid hierarchy of research supremacy among universities.

Not only did research funding from the federal government increase but also—and dramatically—funds from individual donors (nearly half the total) and other organizations (principally foundations and corporations). Fund-raising or "development" has become big business at most institutions, including public ones, during the last quarter century with nearly $20 billion given to higher educational institutions in fiscal year 2003. The major public institutions, which previously relied principally on their state legislatures for appropriations, now find the state supplying less than 20 percent (and some, including Virginia and Vermont, only 8 percent) of their budgets. Most publics, including Purdue, have found it necessary during the past decade to join the privates in seeking outside support, particularly when appropriations fell 2.3 percent in 2003–2004.

The private universities still lead in annual donations, however, with Harvard currently first at nearly $556 million, followed by Stanford at $486 million, and the University of Pennsylvania at nearly $400 million. Currently nineteen American universities (nine of which are "public") are engaged in campaigns to raise at least one billion dollars each. No one has provided a definitive analysis of what such fund-raising costs, either in terms of direct expenses or modified program priorities, yet the costs are enormous. Neither have any responsible voices yet been willing to consider contraction of the enterprise.

The consequence of these funding changes since World War II for colleges and universities can be glimpsed by looking at the endowments of Franklin and Purdue, which were not wildly different when C. H. Hall retired from the former and Victor Albjerg joined the latter, and at Harvard, where I have been a professor for more than thirty years.

Endowments (in 000,000 of dollars)			
	Franklin	Purdue	Harvard
1920	0.4	0.004	6.2
1940	0.8	1.8	139
1960	1.9	5.1	371
1980	11.7	34.4	1,500
2000	83.9	1,400	19,100
2004	69.6	1,200	22,600

DOMINANCE OF THE RESEARCH
UNIVERSITY IDEAL

Despite the dramatic discrepancies in funding illustrated by the endowment figures above, paradoxically the greatest enrollment growth over the last half-century has been at institutions, particularly community colleges and four-year public institutions, that do not have a strong research tradition and mostly do not aspire to attain one. The community colleges, in particular, believe their most important missions are to prepare students for jobs in their neighborhoods and to provide the first two years of college work for others who ultimately seek a four-year college degree. Neither of those goals requires extensive research activity on the part of faculty.

Nonetheless, the remaining higher education sector has embraced the ideal of research as something that it expects of its faculty. They emphasize knowledge with a vengeance with no discussion of virtue. But, the ideal does not reflect reality. Probably no more than a fifth of professors engage regularly in research. Even in "research universities" recent studies reveal that less than 40 percent do so. Nonetheless, the obligatory talk is about "research," not about discovering new ways to teach, implementing ideas more effectively, or even supporting an intellectually rigorous life of the mind. Most university professors today would never spend their summer months camping on Lake Superior and recording their observations on Emerson's essays, as C. H. Hall did. Victor with his four books and numerous articles anticipated this trend toward active research and publication.

Some institutions, in their zeal for "research," have taken to counting, as opposed to reading, analyzing and evaluating, the articles a professor has published as a criterion for promotion. Publication in "peer-reviewed journals" is the coin of the realm for promotion and status. Some professors even list their articles on their résumé in two categories: peer-reviewed journals and other journals. Peer-review, of course, means that colleagues in the same field have judged the piece worthy of publication. That can be a very small group and such articles do not reach the general public in most cases.

Perhaps the easiest way to understand this shift in expectation is to compare the number of courses professors are expected to teach today with what was expected earlier in the twentieth century. Teaching requirements have shrunk dramatically from the four fall and four spring courses that Victor taught at Purdue to the two and two courses now common in many universities, with reduced requirements even in the sciences. In places with doctoral programs where professors have significant responsibilities advising students undertaking research, the requirements are even less. The daily demands on one's time, however, in addition to meeting the classes and advising students, are for "service to the profession." Professors are expected to participate in conferences, write letters of recommendations both for one's own former students and for professors seeking promotion at other universities, prepare applications for funding, respond to inquiries about one's writings, and serve on campus or national committees. Professors in private research universities report spending an average of fifty-seven hours per week on these additional professional obligations. In some fields, particularly the sciences and some professional specialties, lucrative consulting or business opportunities attract professors, often supplying both more compensation and cachet than does their faculty appointment. These and other activities dominate one's schedule, leaving relatively little time during the school year for one's own writing and thinking.

The emergence of research expectations brought a diminished responsibility for advisory and administrative obligations. Unlike Victor and Marguerite Albjerg and their colleagues, faculty are now widely dispersed in many communities, not concentrated in faculty residential enclaves near the campus, and often less likely to entertain their students in their homes either as professional socialization or personal hospitality, while expanded offices of "student services" sponsor more occasions of this sort. Unlike Victor, professors rarely organize convocations with professionals performing; specialized administrative staff do that.

Paradoxically, professional student services became major institutional obligations as in loco parentis declined in the 1960s. Colleges emerged as "full service providers" with specialized administrative personnel hired and assigned to care for both the academic and nonacademic needs of students, concerns previously addressed by faculty. "Student personnel administration" (how to take care of students and their needs) itself became a major field in higher education, complete with doctoral programs in major schools of education, such as Teachers College, Columbia. Other administrative offices proliferated, staffed not principally by faculty as the academic deans and provosts jobs had traditionally been, but by a new breed of "academic administrator." All these changes raised costs and came about as faculty were presumed to be giving much of their time to research. Some actually were.

The model for professorial academic life changed after World War II, primarily because at that time most persons interested in becoming faculty members recognized that they needed extensive graduate work, usually including a doctorate, in order to get a good job. Hence, they enrolled in one of the relatively few places that offered this degree, typically a university where the new ethos of universities as centers of research had taken root first. Ten universities in 1940 accounted for half of all research and engineering funds. By 1963 that number had grown to twenty and by 1990 thirty-two such institutions accounted for half the funds. By the 1990s the Carnegie Foundation for the Advancement of Teaching listed 125 universities as Research I (meaning research-oriented) institutions, a more generous definition of research universities. Membership in the Association of American Universities, an organization of the most research-intensive universities, grew from fourteen in 1900 to sixty-two in 2004.

Thus, graduate students hoping to become faculty in the 1950s and 1960s studied under the direction of their research professor and mentor. As historian Kenneth Lynn observed in 1963, "Everywhere in American life, the professions are triumphant," concluding, "Thorstein Veblen's sixty-year-old dream of a professionally run society has never been closer to realization." This was the model that aspiring faculty carried with them to their jobs: membership in a "triumphant profession" at a research-intensive university with a low teaching load and an emphasis on graduate students. Most of the new faculty would not find jobs in such universities, but they sought the same perquisites in their new institutions. However, the professions' triumphal state was short-lived though intense in the midyears of the century.

The professors in the leading two dozen or so research universities of the 1950s and 1960s were the mandarins who were preparing the new generation of professionals, and, as such, they occupied positions of prestige unknown to their predecessors and unlikely to be achieved by their successors. This generation of faculty who came of age after World War II experienced their careers at a period unique in the history of American higher education. Unlike their predecessors, who were expected to find happiness in genteel poverty and spend their lifetimes at a single institution (C. H. Hall at Franklin and Victor at Purdue), many found good incomes and taught at more than one institution. Many were upwardly mobile white sons of recent immigrants and nearly all in the research universities were either Protestant or, after 1950, Jewish. Many exchanged their institutional affiliations frequently; 25 percent of faculty changed jobs each year in the major growth period of the late 1950s and 1960s. Thus, academics' prime loyalty went to the discipline and to the international cadre of fellow scholars in one's discipline and one's subspecialty, not to the institution that paid one's salary. Scholars' concern was with advancement of knowledge, particularly their own, not with the advancement of the institution.

The intellectual vitality these faculty brought both to their studies and to their institutions contributed powerfully to the eminence of the finest American universities. As this research emphasis became the dominant model for higher education, the culture of academe was no longer tied to specific institutions and scholars' commitment to the profession replaced commitment to the institution. Teaching-oriented faculty took solace in their unions, professional associations, and national meetings of like-minded faculty. Administrators attended innumerable conferences throughout the country, often in Washington, D.C., led by the new breed of quasi academics who "represented" higher education to the Congress and White House administrations from their association offices near Dupont Circle.

And what has been the effect of all this emphasis on research? As former president of Harvard Derek Bok observed in 1996, "whether one looks at the number of Nobel Prize winners, the share of articles in scientific journals, or the frequency with which scientific results, are cited, the United States has plainly had great success in promoting the discovery of new knowledge." Bok is correct in that judgment. The United States has led at the high end of knowledge production.

During the last half century more than half of all Nobel prizes and Fields medals (mathematics awards) have gone to scholars living in the United States, while only four of the ninety-two Nobel prizes went to U.S. residents before World War II. Another example of the preeminence and depth of American research: half of all citations in leading scientific journals in the 1990s were to U.S. scholars. Outside the United States these strengths are recognized as nearly half a million students from other countries come here to study (more would come if we permitted them visas), of whom at least one-third are graduate students. Practically none came before World War II; rather, Americans sought to study in Europe.

Contrary to many European nations, where research is conducted in government-funded organizations and other specialized research institutes in which the director decides which of the researchers gets the money, most scholarly research in the United States occurs in universities. Mostly it is funded through a peer-review system in which other scholars consider proposals by colleagues outside their institution but in their fields and make recommendations to government or other funding agencies as to which projects should be supported. At many of the strongest U.S. institutions a comparable process exists for appointment of professors. This tradition has existed in the United States in reasonably rigorous form since World War II and has brought a measure of accountability to university life. No such process exists on U.S. campuses to assure effectiveness in teaching and learning.

U.S. universities surpass all others in their leadership in research, and this recognition prompts legitimate pride. But on other educational dimensions the public has concerns and, in recent years, has translated them into shrinking budgets for public institutions. Teaching, transmitting the new knowledge garnered through research to students, receives steady criticism. The low academic completion rate provides evidence that many students are not mastering the curriculum. Providing an environment that encourages virtue has nearly vanished from campuses where underage drinking is condoned, cheating and plagiarism are rife, college athletics is plagued with infractions, class attendance is sporadic, and courses without academic content are common. Worrisome issues such as these prompt calls for accountability.

CAMPUSES AS CENTERS OF SOCIAL CONTROVERSY

While enrollments in higher education were increasing and while research was intensifying on many campuses in the postwar years, most remarkably, a third activity, which would seem to be inconsistent with the other achievements, emerged. During this period, the American college campus evolved as a center of social controversy.

Throughout the world, university campuses have often been the site of political demonstrations, but the American examples of the last forty years provide a distinctive set of windows onto the social, political, and cultural changes that have affected this country. From the 1950s when fraternities, sororities, and eating clubs dominated campus social life to the 1960s when black students led civil rights protests, undergraduate life underwent a profound transformation. Movies in the early twenty-first century now portray life in the 1950s as historical costume dramas, evidence of the shift in sensibilities from acquiescence to authority to challenges of it. Much of both the leadership and of the action stimulating these challenges to authority have been found on college campuses beginning in the 1960s. More than organized religion, than the business world, than the established professions such as law or medicine, or even the semiprofessional world of school teaching, higher education has been the institution in the center of the controversies embroiling American society.

First, students attacked authority. Prior to the 1960s, student protests, typically conducted under the influence of alcohol and often resulting in some physical damage to the campus, were attributed to the developmental needs of adolescent males, and the focus was mostly local. But in the early 1960s strong moral concerns dominated student protests, and the objects of attack were both university policies and governmental ones. Unlike the familiar "panty raids" and other pranks of the 1950s, these protests attempted to correct institutional practices that seemed to the students flawed and not befitting American democracy.

The Port Huron statement, initiated by University of Michigan undergraduates, argued that everyone should participate in the decisions that shaped their lives. It became the founding document of Students for a Democratic Society (SDS) in 1962 and of the student protest movement in general. Students at Berkeley in 1964 organized the Free Speech Movement, which argued for the expression of dissident views on the campus. The next major outburst was at Columbia in 1968, where mostly white students protested the university's plan to use city parkland for a gym, thus depriving Harlem residents of their recreation area. These issues rapidly escalated into broader demonstrations across the nation in which students, now often joined by faculty, objected to secret war research being conducted on the campuses. Universities ultimately led the nation in opposing the country's involvement in Vietnam.

Students protest for free speech at the University of California, Berkeley, in 1964. As the turbulent decade continued, universities became critical centers for protests about civil rights, Vietnam, secret government research, and other issues. Campuses led in shifting sexual and social mores. *Courtesy of University Archives, The Bancroft Library, University of California, Berkeley; UARC PIC 24B:1:19*

Major protests, requiring police intervention and some-times resulting in bloodshed, occurred at nearly all the most prestigious universities. The most lethal, however, was in 1970 at Kent State University in Ohio, where the national guard fired and killed four demonstrating students. Two more students were killed at Jackson State in Mississippi ten days later. The civility of these campuses, caricatured as sherry hours of pipe-smoking faculty discussing erudite matters, was shattered.

Second, students played vital leadership roles in the civil rights movement, another attack on authority and also a moral crusade. Black undergraduates in the South attempted to integrate lunch counters and in-terstate buses in the 1950s. Autherine Lucy at the University of Alabama, Charlayne Hunter and Hamilton Holmes at the University of Georgia, James Meredith at the University of Mississippi, all African Americans, led the way at those previously all-white institutions to demand that universities serve all the citizens of their state. By the mid-1960s civil rights organizations, in-cluding the Student Non-Violent Coordinating Commit-tee (generally known as SNCC), which initially included both blacks and whites, began to segregate their mem-bership as "black power" emerged as the dominant emphasis within the civil rights movement.

The loss of Martin Luther King Jr.'s leadership after his assassination in Tennessee in 1968 and the assas-sination of Robert F. Kennedy three months later as he was campaigning for the Democratic nomination for presi-dent left the nation without moral leadership. Richard Nixon aspired to fill this vacuum when he was elected president in the fall. By the time of his resignation in 1974 over improprieties in his reelection campaign and after the indictment and the earlier resignation of his vice president, Spiro Agnew, the nation was also en-during an economic recession. Students seeking exem-plars of moral leadership found them in short supply.

University presidents, who traditionally had been seen as leaders in both knowledge and virtue, failed to deliver. Some died suddenly of the strain (for example, the president of Swarthmore, Courtney Smith, unexpectedly collapsed of a heart attack in the middle of a takeover of the admissions office); others were broken by it; a few struggled on, seeking compromises that partisans inevitably found lacking. Most left their presidencies precipitously after the crises, including Grayson Kirk at Columbia and Nathan Pusey at Harvard. Most of these presidents whose leadership had never been challenged on the grounds of their race, gender, or ethnicity found themselves in the midst of discussions about affirmative action, now required by federal government executive order for those institutions (nearly all) that received federal funds. An outgrowth of the civil rights movement, the executive order required recipients of federal funds to seek and hire persons of color and white women if they were qualified and not adequately represented in the workforce.

Of the two issues the only one that mattered for most institutions was "if they were qualified" as no major institutions had adequate representation in the workforce at senior levels of either minorities or white women. What constituted "qualified"? Was it simply a matter of sufficient peer-reviewed articles? What if the "peers" were all white men who were not interested in new topics, such as studies of gender or race? Did teaching skill count? Did it matter for women and students of color to have faculty who looked like them as role models? If so, were one or two enough? Many faculties who had only a generation before excluded Jews found it extraordinarily difficult to introduce women and persons of color to their senior ranks. As one Ivy League dean remarked in the eighties to a group of colleagues over lunch, "Wasn't it so much easier when we were all alike." Wilson's preference at Princeton for gentlemen over scholars died hard.

By the nineties talk on campuses focused on diversity and its alleged benefits. Few found it easy to articulate those benefits, and some found it difficult to accept them in principle. The U.S. Supreme Court expressed those sentiments in a five-to-four decision in 2003 about admission policies at the University of Michigan Law School. The Court agreed with Michigan that educational benefits did accrue from classes of diverse racial heritage. The Ivy League dean of twenty years before who thought it was easier "when we were all alike" may have been right about "easy" but not about "educational."

Enforcement of affirmative action fell to the Office of Civil Rights in the Department of Health, Education, and Welfare in the sixties. It sought to resolve issues through litigation, if necessary, and ultimately to cut off federal funds to offending institutions, an action so draconian in its effect upon research budgets in universities and upon financial aid for all students that it was rarely used. The negotiation and litigation, however, were a profound disincentive for administrations, which did not want the publicity or the expense of those activities. Nor did they want the groups on the campus, principally women, minorities, and their supporters, to gain attention for their plight or "demands."

By the 1970s, higher education institutions were regularly admitting African Americans, often in very small numbers at previously segregated institutions in the South and in somewhat larger numbers at northern colleges and universities. The proportion of black students attending historically black colleges declined steadily in the last quarter of the twentieth century. However, the numbers enrolled in what came to be known as Historically Black Colleges and Universities (HBCUs) increased slightly but not as much as the number of blacks attending previously predominantly white institutions.

At issue, however, was the kind of experience blacks had on mostly white campuses with almost entirely white faculties and administrations, many of whom were not welcoming to the newcomers. One response, made devastatingly evident in 1969 at Cornell in a widely publicized photograph of black students emerging from the student union with guns, was the organization of "black houses" where only black students lived. This was a college example of the emerging Black Power movement in which African American students sought solidarity with other blacks and excluded all others. More modest but poignant examples were "black tables" in the student cafeterias at which whites were not welcomed, and blacks were ostracized by other blacks if they chose not to eat there. On the curricular side black studies and other ethnic studies programs evolved, first as compensatory efforts to augment the existing courses that did not include material about the black and ethnic experiences. They were often criticized initially for being too ideological and for hiring faculty who did not meet customary criteria.

Not until former university presidents William Bowen and Derek Bok, from Princeton and Harvard respectively, published *The Shape of the River* in 1998 was there a comprehensive analysis of the black undergraduate experience at mostly white selective institutions. Their conclusion was that the blacks generally did well in later life despite their lower entering test scores. The most tantalizing and disturbing finding was that blacks with high entering test scores did not receive as high grades in colleges as their test scores predicted, thus raising questions about the extent to which faculty at these institutions both expected and supported first-rate academic work from black students.

The other major objective of affirmative action was to increase opportunities for women, whose experience in higher education differed in several important respects from that of blacks or other ethnic minorities. In pre–World War II America the high watermark for educated women was the 1920s. At a time when only a few (5 percent) of young people attended college, women constituted 47 percent of undergraduates and 15 percent of the doctoral candidates. They did not reach those percentages again until the mid-1970s. As percentages of the age group attending college rose in the 1930s, the fraction who were women declined.

Families in the 1950s evidently believed it was more important for the son to go to college than the daughter, a hidden legacy perhaps of the massive male enrollment of the GI Bill. Women's participation in the workforce dropped precipitously as men found reasonably well-paying jobs, and the birthrate rose steadily, reaching its height in 1957. Mom was supposed to stay at home.

By the sixties the women's movement was challenging such practices, and women's participation in higher education increased rapidly. By 1982 women were receiving the majority of bachelor's degrees, and by 2002, the majority of doctoral degrees. Women have transformed American middle-class life with careers enabled through their undergraduate and graduate degrees.

Unlike black participation in higher education, where the impetus had come from students, the initial leadership for women in higher education came from female faculty and occasionally female administrators. Frequently they occupied marginalized positions within their institution. These women believed, generally correctly, that they were not being treated as the equals of men with similar qualifications on their campuses. Marguerite's case was egregious but quite common.

Eventually Dr. Marguerite Hall Albjerg, published author and distinguished teacher, was hired in her sixties as an assistant in the Dean of Women's Office at Purdue. Although she enjoyed the job, one of her prime qualifications was that she was the only woman on the staff who was a wife, mother, and grandmother and therefore presumably could communicate with the mothers of Purdue students.

As women grew more numerous and vocal on their campuses, they called their administration's attention to these inequities, and when that brought no relief, they called the Office of Civil Rights at the Department of Health, Education, and Welfare's attention to the matter. That generally did not bring relief either, but it did bring attention. The adoption of Title IX in 1972, whose principal effect has been in expanding women's undergraduate athletics, is one example of changes initiated by pressure but implemented by law.

The fundamental change, however, has been in women's changing expectations for their own lives, first for college and then for career. When I married in 1955 and had a daughter in 1957, it never occurred to me that I would work full-time or even part-time despite the fact that I had done well academically in college, had taught high school more or less successfully, and had acquired a master's degree while I was pregnant. Now most women expect paid employment during some or all of their adult lives, and college is an important place to get the initial set of skills and attitudes that will allow for more remunerative work. Graduate school is even better, particularly for a high prestige professional degree, such as law or medicine. Therefore, women students' demand for undergraduate and graduate degrees has become intense. Admission to the ranks of senior faculty positions at prestigious institutions has been considerably slower.

Slow as American academe has been to admit women to its most prestigious ranks, and I have been a steady critic of its laggardly pace, it has moved more rapidly than most other segments of American society. With that movement has come much Sturm und Drang, which has contributed to the sense of controversy that has engulfed the campuses. Undergraduate women or even women graduate students did not fundamentally challenge traditional male/female relations as the male faculty were dealing with subordinate female students. The dynamic is quite different, however, when the woman is a full professor or senior administrator and she is dealing with male colleagues who have never experienced a professional relationship with a woman in an equal or superior professional position. Until quite recently that was often the experience of the few women in senior positions and of most male faculty and administrators, and managing that transition has been the business of both women and men on campuses during the past thirty years.

When I joined the Harvard faculty as a professor in 1974, nearly 95 percent of the professors were men. Today nearly 16 percent of the full professors are women. When I became dean of the faculty of education in 1981, I was the first woman dean at Harvard since its founding in 1636. There have been two since, and several vice presidents have been women. Both the Ivy League and the Big Ten now have had women presidents, as well as black presidents, a considerable change for institutions that had had only white, male, Christian presidents until Martin Meyerson, a Jew, went to the University of Pennsylvania as president in 1970.

The antiwar protests; the civil rights activism of minorities, particularly blacks; and the women's movement all sprang initially from moral concerns, expressed most vividly by individuals on campuses. Moral outrage at society's inequities is one of youth's great contributions. Their lives are not yet tainted with responsibility and their critiques are often vibrant. Campuses, which contain such concentrations of gifted youth, thus become natural incubators for social protests against realities that do not meet the rhetoric of a democracy.

These activists remind faculty and administrators who have positions of responsibility of their individual and institutional lapses. Often elements of the critique are telling. Yet part of that responsibility is also achieving a balance between protest and progress and in recent decades that has been the task of faculties and administrators in higher education where issues of fairness and respect have been more salient than in many other institutions of society. Senior faculty in the research universities may lead in knowledge creation, but over the past forty years many of their junior colleagues and students, as well as some of them, have led in exploring issues of virtue: fairness, honesty, ingenuity, and teamwork. Tension between knowledge and virtue has exacerbated academic disputes, triggering public calls for accountability at institutions sometimes fraught with conflict.

American colleges and universities before World War II were outside the primary attention span of most Americans. They existed in this isolated position for several reasons: few Americans attended them; teaching the liberal arts seemed unimportant; and their internal life was relatively calm. The situation is dramatically different today: many, both young and old, attend; the institutions provide services the public wants; their research reaches into nearly every corner of American life; and enormous sums of money are spent at them. Furthermore, because they are places where persons of color study with whites and where men and women learn to work together, they are the breeding ground for the new demographic realities of American life. Finally, they remain the entrypoint for good jobs now sought by minorities and women as well as white men. Unimportant institutions can exist in autonomy; important institutions require accountability.

Conclusion

How well have American educational institutions fulfilled their shifting assignments: assimilation, adjustment, access, achievement, and accountability? On the whole schools and colleges have delivered what Americans wanted but never as promptly or as completely as they wished. Impatience is a national trait, one to which policy people are particularly prone. Typically educational practice changes slowly, finally achieving the new objective after it is decades old. Furthermore, the reforms are usually only a partial implementation of the new idea, which often changes substantially the value of the innovation. Such sluggishness, while annoying to the reformers who want immediate results for their new idea, nonetheless insulates us from the dramatic swings of enthusiasm, such as education for cognition only or for self-esteem only, both necessary and thus both to be sought, but in a balance.

Schools and colleges today principally justify their existence by how well they are preparing their students to participate in the economy. Most of the evidence they are inclined to present (or to hide) is based on indicators of student academic learning, an important, though inevitably partial, influence on one's capacity to be productive in the economy. Two important elements are missing here. The first is whether participation in the economy is a sufficient justification for tax-supported education in a democracy. The second is whether measures of academic learning, most commonly tests, are broad enough indicators of what students have gained from their schooling.

Traditionally the goals of education and the more specific task of schooling have been much broader than preparing workers for employment. Both in the United States and elsewhere, education has been seen as the means by which the older generation prepares the younger one to assume responsibilities of adulthood, a much wider role than simple employment. Public schools, especially in a democracy such as ours, have the primary institutional obligation to provide children with the academic skills—particularly literacy, numeracy, and an acquaintance with other disciplines, such as history, science, and the arts—to learn about the world in which they live. In addition, schools typically have had an important role in shaping youngsters' traits and attitudes, such as their ingenuity, integrity, and capacity for hard work both individually and collectively.

A democracy, unlike an authoritarian state, expects participation of its citizens in shaping public opinion and making decisions about governing the nation. That participation needs to be both informed by knowledge and leavened with judgment, fairness, and respect. Educational institutions nurture all those qualities. As Nazi Germany illustrated, knowledge and high culture were insufficient attributes at a time when judgment, fairness, and respect were needed desperately. How much attention should be given to each component of education constitutes the perennial debate engulfing our schools and colleges.

Looking at the report card of American schools today, we find a mixed picture. We have little information on what are probably the most important markers for youngsters' adult lives: their ingenuity, integrity, hard work, and ability to work with others. Instead, we find that drop-out rates in schools serving low-income children seem to be rising, as Houston and other cities reveal, while post-secondary participation rates remain stable in the general population at about two-thirds of high school graduates. Yet a high school graduate whose family is in the top income quartile is more than six times as likely as one from the bottom income quartile to graduate with a bachelor's degree after five years. Gaps in average test scores remain between rich and poor and among the races, though somewhat narrower than previously. Math scores are rising on the SAT and remain steady on the ACT, two key college entrance exams, yet ACT officials report that less than half of the students who took the 2003 ACT were prepared for college-level algebra and only a fourth for college biology. More students are studying an academic curriculum in high school than twenty years ago. Only 14 percent of 1982 high school graduates earned four credits in English, three in social studies, science, and mathematics while 56 percent of 1998 graduates did. An ever-increasing number of students participate in advanced placement courses. Selective colleges regularly report academically stronger freshman classes than their predecessors, yet teacher training students in non-selective institutions (where most future teachers prepare) continue to do poorly on tests of general knowledge. In sum, children from affluent families and neighborhoods where high expectations for academic success are held and where considerable support to achieve them exists do better in school on academic measures than do children from low-income families with few neighborhood supports for these youngsters' academic endeavors. This result should not surprise us.

Despite the slogan of "academic achievement for all," the reality has been that the current metric of school reform, test scores, has become one that directly helps those who have many advantages already and whose schools need relatively little reform. For those without such benefits, much school reform is necessary, but, in a society increasingly stratified by wealth, it has not been easy to make the changes either in schooling or in the community that would facilitate such increased academic learning. Nonetheless, the effort to undertake such changes in opportunities for academic learning is deeply laudable, and in various forms we have been working on this effort at democratizing access to learning for some time.

What we do know is this: in the past schools have achieved the objectives set for them, but it has taken a long time. I am hopeful that we will have the same success with the goals of achievement and accountability. Yet in the case of universal academic achievement, schools cannot accomplish this alone. Their efforts must be supported by the culture in which the students, particularly adolescents, live and which recognizes that the prime business of youth is to get educated.

And what of our colleges and universities? They, too, are subject to many of the same criticisms as our public schools though, as yet, the American public has not been as critical of them. At their best, like the best of the elementary and secondary schools, they are superb. At their worst, they are an embarrassment, if not a tragedy. Their strength is their variety, including many of the finest research centers in the world, and the opportunities that these extraordinarily diverse institutions provide for Americans and other nationals to study an immense range of subjects in an incredible assortment of settings, both full-time and part-time, both at home and on campus, and at all ages. Their weakness is that the very finest of our colleges and universities, which unequivocally lead the world in education, are extremely expensive, and, despite considerable efforts at student financial aid, continue to attract students disproportionately from affluent families, thus failing to draw on the widely distributed talent in the population. Finally, attention to student learning—how to increase it and how to make it the central concern of the institution—sometimes wavers in the face of varying pressures, often fiscal, such as allocation of faculty resources or commitment to nonacademic activities, such as sports. The best American colleges and universities are generating new knowledge that is important in its own right and useful to others while enabling a new generation to become more adept with ideas and admirable as adults.

What the country needs now is enhancement of both the wit and the character of the young, and such efforts should be at the heart of our educational institutional efforts. Wit is a more inclusive term for knowledge than academic achievement. Character includes the secular traits of integrity, ingenuity, and hard work, both individually and collectively, that our democracy needs. Schools and colleges must work together with families, communities, employers, and the media to achieve this integration of wit and character. The nation's failure to attract the majority of its citizens to vote is not the result of illiteracy. When tales of greed and scandal among some of our best-known companies and individuals emerge, these are not failures of numeracy. When computing and back-office jobs migrate to India, this may be a failure of academic skills on the part of American workers. More likely, though, it is a result of lower operating costs abroad and American companies' desire for greater wealth for a few resulting in a lower standard of living for many. When triumphs occur in America, and there are plenty of them, they are often the confluence of academic skills with the attributes of character of hard work, ingenuity, and integrity. We often see these in our scientific and technological accomplishments, in the success of our businesses, in the strength of many communities, and in the generosity of our people.

Where will the force come from to help us achieve this integration of wit and character as goals for our schools and colleges? First, it will come from the public who will begin to hold their institutions, particularly their tax-supported ones, accountable for performance defined in ways that benefit both their own children and everybody else's children. The nation flourishes when all its citizens can participate fully in its public life and in its economic growth. Today the sets of skills associated with schooling are enormously more important for such participation, particularly in economic life, than they were a century ago. That makes improved schooling much more vital for everybody than it was previously.

And how will the public manage to keep its attention on this issue? Here the business community, particularly with the leadership of some prominent CEOs, such as Louis V. Gerstner Jr., formerly of American Express, RJR Nabisco, and IBM, has been both steadfast and helpful. Whether one agrees with each particular recommendation they have favored or not, they have invested their resources of both time and money to keep the issue of improving schooling alive in America. Their efforts have been augmented by many nonprofit groups, which have also been outspoken but typically with specific policy recommendations emanating from their various ideological viewpoints. Most of these efforts, while often lively, offer a single solution to the complex problems of improving schooling for all, such as recruiting bright nontraditional teachers or providing vouchers for low-income children to attend private schools. The media have made some significant efforts to offer more substantive discussions about issues of schooling, though education remains a distant third in priorities for most news organizations with the shifting priorities occupying the number one and two spots (whatever they are at the moment) getting most of the attention. Maintaining public attention on the need for good schooling is critical to helping schools improve.

But if the schools are to improve, how are they to do so? In other fields such as medicine, engineering, or electronics when improvement is sought, as Hugh Burkhardt and Alan Schoenfeld have observed, 5 to 15 percent of their expenditures are devoted to research and development, of which typically 20 percent goes to basic research and 80 percent to development. In education, however, instead of 5 to 15 percent spent on R&D, Congress estimates the expenditure is 0.01 percent. That is not enough.

Anyone comparing ordinary schools and colleges in America in 1900 and the ordinary ones today would be astonished by how much better today's are. Those gains are attributable to deeper understanding of children, institutions, and the role of education in the society, all attributable to the stimulus of public engagement, to educators' knowledge, and to ideas developed through research. They have also benefited from greater funding, a stronger teaching force, and criticism from many sources. Our elementary, secondary, and higher education sectors are getting better, just not as rapidly or as completely as we would like. Let us hope that our successors a century from now will find their educational institutions as much improved then as we find ours compared to those of our predecessors.

Further Reading

THE READER INTERESTED IN PURSUING SOME OF THESE QUESTIONS more thoroughly and with authors whose points of view vary would find several books particularly valuable: Norton Grubb and Marvin Lazerson, *The Education Gospel: The Economic Power of Schooling* (Cambridge, MA: Harvard University Press, 2004); Jennifer Hochschild and Nathan Scovronick, *The American Dream and the Public Schools* (New York: Oxford University Press, 2003); two books by Diane Ravitch, *The Troubled Crusade: American Education 1945–1980* (New York: Basic, 1983) and *Left Back* (New York: Simon & Schuster, 2000); David B. Tyack and Larry Cuban, *Tinkering toward Utopia* (Cambridge, MA: Harvard University Press, 1995); and David B. Tyack, *Seeking Common Ground* (Cambridge, MA: Harvard University Press, 2003). Ellen Condliffe Lagemann's *An Elusive Science: The Troubling History of Educational Research* (Chicago: University of Chicago Press, 2000) clarifies the role of that murky subject and its influence on educational practice. David Labaree's *The Trouble with Ed Schools* (New Haven, CT: Yale University Press, 2004) updates Geraldine Joncich Clifford and James Guthrie's *Ed School: A Brief for Professional Education* (Chicago: University of Chicago Press, 1988) in explaining the role of schools of education in preparing educators. The companion research volume to this book in the Institutions of Democracy series, which readers seeking fuller understanding of these issues would find useful, is Susan Fuhrman and Marvin Lazerson, eds., *The Public Schools* (New York: Oxford University Press, 2005).

The standard history of American schooling for the first half of the twentieth century remains Lawrence A. Cremin's *The Transformation of the School: Progressivism in American Education, 1876–1957* (New York: Knopf, 1961). Just before his death, he supplemented this work in a series of lectures at Harvard published as *Popular Education and Its Discontents* (New York: Harper & Row, 1990). The third volume of Cremin's trilogy, *American Education: The Metropolitan Experience, 1876–1980* (New York: Harper & Row, 1988), provides an exhaustive bibliography for the period though does not include much discussion of either government activities or of racial issues involving education. Richard Kluger's *Simple Justice* (New York: Knopf, 1976) is the classic treatment of the history of the latter subject. A new edition published in 2004 provides a supplementary chapter covering events since the initial publication.

ASSIMILATION: 1900–1920

Leonard Ayres, *Laggards in Our Schools* (New York: Russell Sage, 1909), portrays the reality of schooling in this period with remarkable accuracy. Those seeking to understand more about schooling in America during this time might wish to begin with John Dewey's early and clearest essays on the subject, "The School and Society" (1899) and "The Child and the Curriculum" (1902). Those venturing further into Dewey's thought should delve into his major statement, *Democracy and Education: An Introduction to the Philosophy of Education* (1916), and for those interested in his later thoughts on the subject, *Experience and Education* (1938). Each has been republished several times.

Several good biographies of John Dewey exist, including Robert B. Westbrook, *John Dewey and American Democracy* (Ithaca, NY: Cornell University Press, 1991). The activities of another influential educator of the era but one with a more limited set of interests, Edward L. Thorndike of Teachers College, Columbia University, are recounted in Geraldine Joncich, *The Sane Positivist: A Biography of Edward L. Thorndike* (Middletown, CT: Wesleyan University Press, 1968). The testing expert Lewis Terman is the focus of Paul Davis Chapman, *Schools as Sorters: Lewis M. Terman, Applied Psychology and the Intelligence Testing Movement, 1890–1930* (New York: New York University Press, 1988). Victor L. Albjerg prepared an unpublished autobiographical essay, "An Adventure in American Education," (circa 1970), on deposit in Special Collections, Purdue University Library, West Lafayette, Indiana.

ADJUSTMENT: 1920–1954

Contemporary accounts of the adjustment era include: Harold Rugg and Ann Shumaker, eds., *The Child Centered School: An Appraisal of the New Education* (Chicago: World Book, 1928); Caroline Ware, *Greenwich Village: A Comment on American Civilization in the Post-War Years* (Boston: Houghton Mifflin, 1935); George S. Counts, *Dare the School Build A New Social Order?* (New York: John Day, 1932); and the publications of the U.S. Office of Education Life Adjustment Commission, particularly *Life Adjustment Education for Every Youth* (n.d.) and *Vitalizing Secondary Education: Report of the First Commission on Life Adjustment Education for Youth* (1951). The summary account of the Eight Year Study is Wilford M. Aikin, *The Story of the Eight-Year Study* (New York: McGraw Hill, 1942). Scanning the journals *Progressive Education* (1924–1957) and *The Social Frontier* (1934–1939) provides a lively review of current thinking about education as do the education articles in *The New Republic* for this period.

More recent analyses of this period include Joyce Antler's excellent biography, *Lucy Sprague Mitchell: The Making of a Modern Woman* (New Haven, CT: Yale University Press, 1987). Other useful recent biographies include Morris Finder, *Educating America: How Ralph W. Tyler Taught America to Teach* (Westport, CT: Praeger, 2004); J. Wesley Null, *A Disciplined Progressive Educator: The Life and Career of William Chandler Bagley* (New York: Peter Lang, 2003); and the compilation of brief life histories of educators in the 1971 volume of the *National Society for the Study of Education (NSSE) Yearbook* (Chicago: University of Chicago Press, 1971).

ACCESS: 1954–1983

The most vivid portraits of schooling in the mid-twentieth century reveal its difficulties, most dramatically in the "educational protest literature" cited in this chapter. If one were to read a single volume on this subject, Arthur Bestor's *Educational Wasteland: The Retreat from Learning in Our Public Schools* (Urbana: University of Illinois Press, 1953) would convey the spirit of the times. James B. Conant excoriated secondary education in *The American High School Today* (New York: McGraw Hill, 1959), and continued with the problems of teacher education in *The Education of American Teachers* (New York: McGraw Hill, 1963). Jonathan Kozol recognized the particular problems of schooling for poor and minority children in *Death at an Early Age: The Destruction of the Hearts and Minds of Negro Children in the Boston Public Schools* (Boston: Houghton Mifflin, 1967). Charles Silberman followed with a comprehensive indictment of schooling in *Crisis in the Classroom: The Remaking of American Education* (New York: Random House, 1970). Contemporary with these critiques was a group of writers who claimed that schooling itself as currently practiced was bad for children. Among these were A. S. Neil, *Summerhill: A Radical Approach to Child Rearing* (New York: Hart, 1960); Paul Goodman, *Growing Up Absurd: Problems of Youth in the Organized System* (New York: Random House, 1960); James Herndon, *The Way It Spozed to Be* (New York: Simon & Schuster, 1968); and Ivan Illich, *Deschooling Society* (New York: Harper & Row, 1971).

Funded by outside agencies concerned about education, social scientists began to address issues of schooling. Psychologist Jerome Bruner was a leader among them with his *The Process of Education* (Cambridge, MA: Harvard University Press, 1960), which laid the basis for revisions of the school curriculum that would serve primarily "gifted and talented" students. Sociologist James S. Coleman examined the school experience of principally low-income children in his report for the U.S. Office of Education, *Equality of Educational Opportu-*

nity (Washington, DC: Government Printing Office, 1966), and had his findings reexamined in a seminar led by statistician Frederick Mosteller and sociologist Daniel Patrick Moynihan and edited as *On Equality of Educational Opportunity* (New York: Vintage, 1972). Sociologist Christopher Jencks and a group of colleagues (Marshall Smith, Henry Acland, Mary Jo Bane, David Cohen, Herbert Gintis, Barbara Heyns, and Stephan Michelson) brought out *Inequality: A Reassessment of the Effect of Family and Schooling in America* (New York: Basic, 1972), which documented the differences in quality of schooling and of academic achievement of the rich and the poor in America. Historian John Rudolph provides a penetrating analysis of scholars' efforts to improve schooling in *Scientists in the Classroom: The Cold War Reconstruction of American Science Education* (New York: Palgrave, 2002).

Gunnar Myrdal's *An American Dilemma: The Negro Problem and American Democracy* (New York: Harper & Row, 1944) set the stage for the understanding of race issues in America. Now literature about desegregation abounds, including biographies of leaders in the NAACP's efforts to overturn legal segregation of the races in schools. The best recent summary of these events is James T. Patterson, *Brown v. Board of Education: A Civil Rights Milestone and Its Troubled Legacy* (New York: Oxford University Press, 2001). J. Anthony Lukas provides a compelling narrative of a northern city's (Boston's) efforts to desegregate its schools in *Common Ground: A Turbulent Decade in the Lives of Three American Families* (New York: Knopf, 1985).

Recent biographies of John F. Kennedy, particularly Robert Dallek, *An Unfinished Life: John F. Kennedy, 1917–1963* (Boston: Little Brown, 2003), and of Lyndon B. Johnson, especially Robert A. Caro, *Master of the Senate: The Years of Lyndon Johnson* (New York: Knopf, 2002), provide insight into the presidency and its involvement with educational issues. Joseph A. Califano Jr.'s autobiography, *Inside: A Public and Private Life* (New York: Public Affairs, 2004) includes revealing anecdotes about education from his insider role in both the Johnson and Carter administrations. Hugh Davis Graham brings his historical skills to these issues in *The Uncertain Triumph: Federal Education Policy in the Kennedy and Johnson Years* (Chapel Hill: University of North Carolina Press, 1984).

ACHIEVEMENT: 1983–PRESENT

A Nation at Risk, written by the Commission on Excellence in Education chaired by David Gardner and published by the Government Printing Office in 1983, unleashed a string of studies pointing to American students' academic deficiencies and schools' failures to create hospitable environments for learning. Others among them of particular interest include *Making the Grade* (New York: Twentieth Century Fund, 1983); Ernest L. Boyer, *High School: A Report on Secondary Education in America* (New York: Harper & Row, 1983); Theodore R. Sizer, *Horace's Compromise: The Dilemma of the American High School* (Boston: Houghton Mifflin, 1984); and Arthur G. Powell, Eleanor Farrar, and David K. Cohen, *The Shopping Mall High School: Winners and Losers in the Educational Marketplace* (Boston: Houghton Mifflin, 1985). Anthony Bryk, Valerie Lee, and Peter Holland in *Catholic Schools and the Common Good* (Cambridge, MA: Harvard University Press, 1993) emphasize the importance of a defining purpose in those schools, a quality many American public schools lost in the latter half of the twentieth century. Bryk's most recent volume with Barbara Schneider, *Trust in Schools* (New York: Russell Sage, 2002), stresses the importance of trust, as opposed to regulation, in school life. David K. Cohen and Heather Hill address regulatory issues in *Learning Policy: When State Education Reform Works* (New Haven, CT: Yale University Press, 2001). Following current issues surrounding schooling can best be done by reading the periodical *Education Week* and by visiting the websites of the Public Education Network (www.publiceducation.org) and the Thomas Fordham Foundation (www.edexcellence.net).

AUTONOMY TO ACCOUNTABILITY

The best recent historical book on American higher education is Julie A. Reuben, *The Making of the Modern University: Intellectual Transformation and the Marginalization of Morality* (Chicago: University of Chicago Press, 1996). Earlier standards, which are still valuable for their twentieth-century discussions, include: Richard Hofstadter and Walter Metzger, *The Development of Academic Freedom in the United States* (New York:

Columbia University Press, 1955); Laurence Veysey, *The Emergence of the American University* (Chicago: University of Chicago Press, 1965); and Clark Kerr, *The Uses of the University* (New York: Harper & Row, 1966).

Institutional histories dominate the historical literature about higher education, and some are very good. Merle Curti and Vernon Carstensen led the group for state universities with their study, *The University of Wisconsin: A History* (Madison: University of Wisconsin Press, 1949). More recently Richard Freeland's *Academia's Golden Age: Universities in Massachusetts, 1945–1970* (New York: Oxford University Press, 1992) and Rosalind Rosenberg's *Changing the Subject: How the Women of Columbia Shaped the Way We Think about Sex and Politics* (New York: Columbia University Press, 2004) illuminate particular issues facing institutions.

William Bowen and Derek Bok, *The Shape of the River: Long-Term Consequences of Considering Race in College and University Admissions* (Princeton, NJ: Princeton University Press, 2000) provides the most comprehensive understanding of the experience of minority students on selective college campuses. Both authors have continued to write about higher education, particularly William Bowen with James Shulman on athletics, *The Game of Life: College Sports and Educational Values*, (Princeton, NJ: Princeton University Press, 2001), and with Martin Kurzweil and Eugene Tobin, *Equity and Excellence in American Higher Education* (Charlottesville: University of Virginia, 2005). Derek Bok, *Universities in the Marketplace: The Commercialization of Higher Education* (Princeton, NJ: Princeton University Press, 2003) captures the present dilemmas of autonomy and accountability.

Index

Page numbers in *italics* refer to illustrations.

Purdue University, 209, *210–11*, 217, 229–32, 234
Purpose of schooling, 1–6, 249–55; Americanization, 7–11, 14–15, *17*, 23, 27, 45, 161; knowledge, 5–6, 10, 19, 22, 45, 50, 60, 76, 80, 93, 103, 106, 116–17, 126, 160–61, 200, 230, 236, 250, 253–54; life adjustment, 53–56, 62, 76–77, 91–92, 160; mobility, 9, 11, 20, 97, 102, 144, 160; preparation for work, 15, 20, 41–43, 76, 162–63, 166, 176, 205, 225, 249; virtue, 5–6, 10–11, 14, 18–19, 22, 41, 45, 50, 60, 64, 76, 80, 93, 103, 106, 116–17, 126, 160–61, 200, 230, 236, 250, 253–54
Pusey, Nathan, 240

Rand Corporation, 182. 193, 195
Ravitch, Diane, 66, 168, 199
Reagan, Ronald, 151, 153, *154*, 156–57, 162, 184, 199
Reed, James, 49
Research, educational, 86–88, 90, 92, 108–9, 117–19, 124–25, 140–41, 143–46, 155, 195–200, 221, 255; funding, 195, 198–200, 204, 228–29, 233, 235, 246, 255; university, 6, 204, 206–7, 211–14, 221–25, 227–36, 246, 252
Richardson, Elliot, 108, 136, 138
Richman, Julia, 57

Rickover, Hyman, 113–14, 169
Riis, Jacob, 23
Riles, Wilson, 130
Rivlin, Alice, 225
Rockefeller Foundation, 181
Rotberg, Iris, 146
Rudolph, John, 121
Rugg, Harold, 53
Rush, Benjamin, 18

San Antonio v. *Rodriguez,* 147
San Francisco State Normal School, 68
Scaife Foundations, 181
Scheffler, Israel, 118
Schoenfeld, Alan, 255
Schools of education, 31–32, 34, 55, 58, 60–61, 68–70, 81–88, 92–94, 96–97, 112–19, 123–26, 139, 174, 192–96, 207, 219
Scott, Hugh, 130
SDS (Students for a Democratic Society), 237
Segregation, 1, 18–22, 82–83, *89*, 98–100, 102–3, 106, 114, 127–28, 133, 136–38, 164–65, 213, 219, *220. See also* Desegregation
Servicemen's Readjustment Act of 1944. *See* GI Bill
Seven Cardinal Principles, 76–78, 80, 85, 92, 99, 127
Shanker, Albert, 171, *172,* 173–74, 187
Short, Luther, 35–36
Shumaker, Ann, 53
Silberman, Charles, 114
Simkhovitch, Mary, 57

PATRICIA GRAHAM IS ONE OF AMERICA'S MOST ESTEEMED HISTORIANS OF EDUCATION, FORMERLY DEAN OF HARVARD'S Graduate School of Education and Director of the National Institute of Education. In this informative volume, Graham offers a vibrant history of American education in the last century.

Drawing on a wide array of sources, from government reports to colorful anecdotes, Graham skillfully illustrates Americans' changing demands for our schools, and how schools have responded by providing what critics want, though never as completely or as quickly as they would like.

In 1900, as waves of immigrants swept the nation, the American public wanted schools to assimilate students into American life, combining the basics of English and arithmetic with emphasis on patriotism, hard work, fair play, and honesty. In the 1920s, the focus shifted from schools serving a national need to serving individual needs; education was to help children adjust to life. By 1954 the emphasis moved to access, particularly for African-American children to desegregated classrooms, but also access to special programs for the gifted, the poor, the disabled, and non-English speakers. Now Americans want achievement for all, defined as higher test scores. The public largely ignored colleges until after World War II when research received international recognition and enrollments grew.